ATHENS

Hints for using the Guide

Following the tradition established by Karl Baedeker in 1844, buildings, places of natural beauty and sights of particular interest are distinguished by one ★ or two ★★ stars.

To make it easier to locate the various places listed in the Sights from A to Z section of the guide, their coordinates on the large map included with the guide are shown in red at the head of each entry.

Coloured strips down the outside edge of the right-hand pages are an aid to finding the different sections of the guide. Blue indicates the introductory material, red the descriptions of sights, and yellow the practical information at the end of the book.

Only a selection of hotels and restaurants can be given: no reflection is implied, therefore, on establishments not included.

In a time of rapid change it is difficult to ensure that all the information given is entirely accurate and up to date, and the possibility of error can never be entirely eliminated. Although the publishers can accept no responsibility for inaccuracies and omissions, they are always grateful for corrections and suggestions for improvement.

Preface

This guide to Athens is one of the new generation of Baedeker guides. These guides, illustrated throughout in colour, are designed to meet the needs of the modern traveller. They are quick and easy to consult, with the principal places of interest described in alphabetical order, and the information is presented in a format that is both attractive and easy to follow.

The guide is in three parts. The first part presents a general survey of Athens, its topography, climate, population, economy, history, famous people and architecture. A selection of quotations leads on to the second part, in which the individual sights and features of interest are described. The third part contains a variety of practical information. Both the Sights from A to Z and the Practical Information sections are in alphabetical order.

The Odeion of Herodes Atticus

Baedeker guides are noted for their concentration on essentials and their convenience of use. They contain numerous colour illustrations and specially drawn plans, and at the end of the book is a fold-out map, making it easy to locate the various places described in the Sights from A to Z section with the help of the coordinates given at the head of each entry.

Contents

Nature, Culture, History
9–35

Sights from A to Z
36–119

Practical Information from A to Z
120–154

Baedeker Specials

From Polis

From the Acropolis, once a fortress mountain and then the place of worship of Athena Parthenos, you can look across the antique sites, the temples, the wandering halls on the Agora, across the residential and commercial buildings on the surrounding hills of Attica, right to the harbour of Piraeus, and the words of the statesman Péricles come to mind, "Our constitution is called a democracy ... we love beauty and the sciences ... Thus the Athenian state is a high school for the whole of Greece."

Athens is considered to be the original Greek *polis* (or city state) without whom our European urban culture would be unthinkable. Today, the negative aspects of urban life, business, milling crowds, traffic noise and smog, sometimes dominate in the Greek capital, but one should not forget the properties embodied by Athena, the patron goddess of this town: wisdom, beauty and fighting spirit. The Athenian philosophers, be it Socrates, Plato or Aristotle, reflected upon the origins of the world, the meaning of divinity, the essence of humanity and the social organisation of human beings. The works of the great dramatists Aischylos, Sophocles, Euripides and Aristophanes are still performed on the stage today. Beauty still emanates from the creations of the architects, sculptors and potters of antiquity. The buildings of the Acropolis are unique, especially the columnar marble temple of Athena Parthenos which, from all sides, represents the petrified harmony of measure and number. The expansive area of the Agorá impresses with its ruins of temples, assembly and wander-

Acropolis and Agora
Centres of the classical town

Theatre of Dionysos
Birthplace of European theatre

to Metropolis

ing halls. Master works of human representation in figure and relief are on show at the Acropolis Museum, with its references to everyday life, as well as at the National Archaeological Museum which has magnificent finds from all over Greece.

After the Persian Wars and the battle for Sparta, the Athenian fighting spirit had given way to resignation. Alexander the Great, Roman emperors and Byzantine rulers brought little new glamour to Athens, and the subsequent almost 400-year Turkish rule left its traces only in the culture of everyday life. After the war of liberation and the foundation of the new Greek state, in 1834, Athens finally advanced from a provincial town to the capital of the Hellenes, home to the king's residence and the seat of parliament. The small town was transformed into a metropolis with open squares, magnificent boulevards, public buildings and residential houses in the Classicist style. In the 20th century, the political fate of the capital was changeable: occupation during World War II, military dictatorship and finally the return of democracy. Apparently, the Athenians were able to let all these events march past with a certain composure. *Joie de vivre* always dominates, despite housing shortages and worries about unemployment, when on a warm summer's evening one shares a meal with friends in a taverna in the Pláka district, under a starry sky and in full view of the beautifully lit Acropolis.

Zeus
In the National Archaeology Museum

Academy of Sciences
The classical building represents modern Athens

Pláka
The inviting old town

Nature, Culture History

Facts and Figures

*Arms of the City
of Athens*

General

Athens (Greek Athína) is the capital of the Hellenic Republic of Greece as well as the chief town of the administrative district (Greek nómos) of Attica.

The city, which has contributed so much to Western culture ever since ancient times, is now the spiritual and financial centre of Greece. As well as being the seat of the head of the Greek Orthodox Church it houses a university and other educational establishments, together with museums of world renown.

Location

Athens lies in longitude 24° 43' east and latitude 37° 58' north on the Saronic Gulf, on the south coast of the mountainous peninsula of Attica stretching to the south-east.

The city is bounded on the east by the 1027m (3375 ft) high Hymettos ridge, on the north-east by the Pentelikon (1110 m (3650 ft)), to the north-

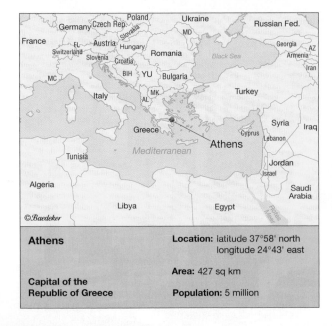

Athens	Location: latitude 37°58' north longitude 24°43' east
	Area: 427 sq km
Capital of the Republic of Greece	Population: 5 million

west by the Parnes (1413 m (4645 ft)) and to the west by the Aegaleos Mountains, which rise to a height of 467 m (1535 ft).

Other landmarks visible within the city boundaries are the Acropolis (156 m (512 ft) above sea-level), the very core of Athens, the Pnyx (110 m (362 ft)) and, last but not least, the Lykabettos (277 m (910 ft)). All three are mountains of cretaceous chalk. The fluvial plains of Ilissos and Kifissos lie to the west.

About 8 km (5 mi.) south-west of the city centre a rocky peninsula enters the Saronic Gulf, forming the natural harbour of Piraeus.

Greater Athens has an area of 427 sq. km (165 sq. mi.), stretching from the slopes of the Parnes and the Pentelikon down to the Saronic Gulf and the Attica Riviera. It measures some 30 km (19 mi.) from south-west to north-east, and up to 20 km (13 mi.) from north-west to south-east.
Area

The population is currently 4 million, equivalent to 9,368 per sq. km (24,242 per sq. mi.).

30 per cent of all Greek industrial firms are to be found in Greater Athens, as well as 40 per cent of all the motor vehicles licensed in Greece.

With its banks, commerce and industry, airport and freight-handling facilities (e.g. the port of Piraeus), the Athens of today occupies a leading economic position in the eastern Mediterranean. Greater Athens has a population of some four million, representing 40 per cent of the total for the whole of Greece.
Financial centre

The climate of Athens is governed by the relatively low rainfall, which for years has averaged only 400 mm (16 in) per annum, July to September being particularly dry. Rain can be expected on about 100 days of the year in all, falling mainly between the end of October and early February. Snow can be anticipated on four or five days in winter.
Climate

From December to February temperatures average between 9.6°C (49.3°F) and 11.4°C (52.5°F), with some frosty days when it may fall to as low as −5.5°C (22°F). From May to September the average temperatures lie between 20.5°C (69°F) and 28°C (82.4°F), sometimes soaring to more than 40°C (104°F) in high summer.

Athens enjoys about 2,700 hours of sunshine each year, mainly between April and October. The interchange of air brought about by its proximity to the sea guarantees a favourable climate.

Unrestricted population growth, rapid industrialisation and, above all, the huge increase in the use of motor vehicles in Athens – from 214,000 in 1970 to some 900,000 in 1990 – have all resulted in serious environmental problems.
Environment

The Athens smog, causing damage to buildings and endangering human life, has become notorious. As a result the law now states that cars and taxis must take it in turns to use the city streets between 8am and 8pm, i.e. number plates ending in an even number on one day and odd numbers the next. About 50 streets and squares in the city centre are largely barred to traffic.

Free local public transport in the early morning is expected to help to reduce the use of private cars. The irresponsible use of aerosols is threatening the fabric of ancient buildings and is presenting conservationists with almost insoluble problems.

Contamination of public water supplies has also become a matter of great concern in the Athens area, and numerous attempts have been made to improve the quality of the water in the Saronic Gulf. It is not unusual to find that bathing is prohibited in many resorts near to the city, so bathers are recommended to avoid the vicinity of Piraeus harbour.

Athens lies within the district of Attica (Nómos), of which it is the administrative centre. Greater Athens is divided into the municipal regions of
Local administration

Athens, Piraeus, West Attica and East Attica, and includes 57 sub-districts (dimos) each with its own council offices. The port of Piraeus, with 200,000 inhabitants, Peristerion with 150,000 and Kallithea with 120,000 all enjoy autonomous municipal authority.

Population

Almost a quarter of the total population of Greece lives in the Athens area. Only a hundred years ago the town had no more than 124,000 inhabitants, compared with the 5 million people who now live in Greater Athens. It is estimated that some two out of every three Athenians come from the islands, from the villages on the Greek mainland or from Asia Minor.

The Greeks feel themselves to be the descendants of the Greeks of classical antiquity, but as a result of their many centuries of foreign rule their blood is mixed with that of many other peoples (Turks, Albanians, Bulgars, etc.).

Athens is home to many peoples, including Turks, Slavs, Vlachs, Albanians, Pomaks, Bulgarians, Armenians and gipsies.

Religion

In spite of the regional differences resulting from the vicissitudes of history and the country's extreme geographical fragmentation the Greeks have preserved a strong sense of their national identity. One great unifying force, particularly in times of hardship and oppression, has been the Orthodox Church, which is still a major influence in both the personal and the public life of the Greeks. The Greek church has been autonomous since 1833; since 1850 it has been recognised by the Oecumenical Patriarchate in Constantinople as autocephalous (appointing its own patriarchs); and since 1864 it has been the national ("established") Church of Greece.

The Greek Orthodox Church has 82 dioceses, the bishops of which are known as metropolitans. The Archbishop of Athens and All Greece is also the head of the Greek Church and presides over the Holy Synod, a permanent body of ten members, and over meetings of the "hierarchs" of the Church. Normally parish priests are married.

The great majority of the population of Greece (97 per cent) belong to the Greek Orthodox Church. There are also small groups – mainly foreigners – of Roman Catholics, Protestants, Jews and Moslems, as well as a variety of sects. All these religious minorities enjoy freedom of worship.

Industry

At present more than 350,000 workers are employed with small industrial and craft firms operating in the Greater Athens area. In the main, these manufacturing firms supply only the needs of the Athens area and the Greek domestic market, although some – especially textile and leather goods industries – do aim at the export market.

Most of the 50,000 or so firms are very small, employing five people at the most.

Branches of
industry

The main forms of industry found in the secondary sector are textile and leather goods, mining, foodstuffs and semi-luxury foods and tobacco, motor vehicles, machinery and metalworking, shipbuilding, woodworking, paper and printing and – last but not least – the chemical industry.

The market hall offers a wide variety of food

The larger industrial sites are found mainly on the south-western edge of the city, at the port of Piraeus and on the Bay of Eleusis.

The main pillar of the Athenian economy is the tertiary sector, comprising head offices of large companies, banks, insurance companies and numerous wholesale and retail firms. More than half of all Greek imports value-wise and more than half of the country's exports pass through the port of Piraeus or Elliniko airport. In the wake of the large industrial firms solicitors, economic and tax advisers, assessing bureaux and the like have also become established in the city.

Service industries

Tourism should not be underestimated as an economic factor. Most visitors to Greece – about 8,400,000 in 1989 – stay or at least stay over in or near Athens, and its world-famous historical sites and museums attract huge numbers of tourists every year; more than 1,200,000 throng to the Acropolis alone. During the last twenty years or so this has resulted in an enormous growth in the number of hotels and guest-houses in Athens and in the charming coastal sectors of Attica.

Tourism

Transport

Ellinikon Airport near Athens is one of the most important international airports, with over 100,000 starts and landings each year. Some eleven million passengers checked in in 1990, in addition to which more than 80,000 tonnes of air freight are loaded annually, together with more than eight million letters and parcels. The East Airport is used only by international airlines. The West or National Airport handles all services flown by the national airline, Olympic Airways.

Airports

Culture

Ports

The port of Piraeus is the most important in Greece and one of the busiest in the eastern Mediterranean. It handles some 14 million tonnes of goods in the course of a year, including most of Greece's imports and exports. It is the starting-point of boat services to all the Greek islands and to the whole of the eastern Mediterranean. Almost all the cruisers operating in the Mediterranean call regularly at Piraeus. Every year more than five million passengers pass through Piraeus, most of them between May and September.

An alternative port is that of Páleo Fáliro, from where excursion ships and hydrofoils depart for the nearer islands in the Saronic Gulf and the Aegean. A further harbour has been constructed at Rafina, in the Gulf of Euboa, east of Athens.

Bus services

Athens lies at the centre of the network of domestic bus services that link the city with towns and villages throughout the country.

There are also the bus services run by the State Railways. Within the city and suburbs of Athens there are trolleybuses, and buses.

Railways

The main station of Athens, the Larissa Station (Stathmós Larissis), is on the State Railways line from Piraeus via Athens to Salonica and Alexandroúpolis. Modern Inter-City trains ply between Athens and Salonica. The Peloponnese Station is on the narrow-gauge Peloponnese Railway, which runs from Piraeus via Athens to Corinth and south through the Peloponnese to Kalamáta.

Electric Railway

This provides a fast service, running underground for part of the way, from Piraeus through central Athens to Kifissiá in the north.

Motorways

Athens is the starting point of motorways (expressways) to the north and west of Greece and to the Peloponnese.

Culture

Athens is the cultural centre of Greece, with its University and College of Technology, the Academy of Sciences, a Commercial College and Academy of Art, several libraries, including the National Library (photograph below) and the Gennadiós Library, a specialised library on Greece, and a whole range of museums of ancient and Byzantine culture, art galleries and natural history collections.

Athens is also the headquarters of the Greek Archaeological Society and a number of foreign archaeological institutes.

Education

The educational reform of 1964 introduced free and compulsory schooling for six years from the age of six. The new constitution of 1975 provided for a nine-year period of compulsory schooling. In practice this has long been in operation.

Festivals

The Athens Festival is held annually in July–September in the Odeion of Herodes Atticus (see A to Z). The programme includes operatic and dramatic performances and concerts by leading Greek and international orchestras.

Theatres

Athens has some 40 theatres. A knowledge of modern Greek is, of course, necessary to appreciate the performances.

One of the few Karagiosis theatres still operating is the Hardimos theatre near the Monument of Lysikrátous (see A to Z). These shadow plays, derived from the Turkish Karagîz ("Black-Eye"), are played with coloured leather figures representing stock types.

Cinemas

Many cinemas in Greece are open-air. Foreign films are usually shown in the original with Greek subtitles.

History

Mythology

Athens, aware of its high antiquity, honoured a series of mythical kings as its earliest rulers. According to the tradition recorded by Apollodorus and others the first king of Athens was Kekrops (c. 1580 BC), who had the body of a snake and was credited with the first census of the population, the first laws, the introduction of monogamy and the invention of the alphabet. In his reign took place the contest between Poseidon and Athena for the land of Attica, a contest from which Athena emerged victorious. The tomb of Kekrops was incorporated into the Erechtheion (see A to Z, Acropolis) and is now under the Caryatid Porch. Close by is an olive-tree, marking the spot where Athena is said to have planted the first olive-tree.

Kekrops was followed by Kranaos, who ruled at the time of the great Grecian flood. After ruling for twelve years he was expelled by Erichtonios, a son of Hephaistos and Athena the Earth Mother. He took the form of a snake. Raised by Athena, he erected wooden statues to the goddess and founded the Pathenaic festival.

The sixth king was Pandion's son Erechtheus, whose stronghold is mentioned by Homer (Il, 7, 81). His twin brother Boutes was a priest of Athena and Poseidon, whose cult was later celebrated in the Erechtheion. Erechtheus was succeeded by his descendants Kekrops II and Pandion II, the latter of whom was driven out and fled to Megara. His son Aegeus returned to Athens. The Aegean Sea is named after Aegeus, who threw himself into the sea when he saw the Athenian fleet returning with black sails and believed that his son Theseus' expedition had been unsuccessful.

This Theseus, the great hero of Athens, was the tenth of the mythical kings. The bringing together of the whole population of Attica in the city state of Athens (the "synoecism") is attributed to him. Travelling from Troizen, his birthplace, along the Saronic Gulf to Athens, he destroyed a series of robbers and monsters like Procrustes; and by killing the Minotaur he ended the payment of tribute by Athens to the Cretan king Minos. With his friend Peirithoos he fought the centaur, with Herakles he fought the Amazons. He carried off the young Helen from Sparta to Aphidna in Attica. Finally he was killed on the island of Skyros by his host, king Lykomedes. About 475 BC Kimon brought his remains to Athens and built the Theseion in his honour.

The last king of Theseus' line was Thymoites, who passed on the crown to Melanthos, who had been driven out of Pylos by the invading Dorians, in gratitude for his military help. Melanthos was succeeded by his son Kodros, whose sacrificial death in 1068 BC saved Athens from the Dorian attack.

According to one tradition Kodros was the last of the kings. According to others he was succeeded by his son Medon, while other sons initiated the Greek settlement of the W coast of Asia Minor, Neleus being honoured as the founder of Miletus, Androklos as the founder of Ephesus.

These mythical traditions reflect the history of Athens from the early Mycenaean period to the beginning of the 1st millennium BC. The history of the site, however, reaches much further back in time.

Chronology

First traces of settlement on the southern slopes of the Acropolis and in   c. 3000 BC

15

Chronology

	the Agora area. These pre-Greeks were traditionally known as "Pelasgians".
c. 2000 BC	Indo-European peoples move into the Aegean mainland area and subjugate the Pre-Greeks.
c. 1400 BC	The Acropolis becomes a fortified royal citadel covering an area of 35,000 sq. m – 378,000 sq. ft (Mycenae 30,000 sq. m – 324,000 sq. ft, Tiryns 20,000 sq. m – 216,000 sq. ft).
1200 BC	The Dorians bypass Attica. Athens takes in refugees from the Peloponnese. Population pressure leads to the establishment of colonies in western Asia Minor and on the islands off its coasts.
9th *c.* BC	The noble families of Attica take up residence in Athens.
8th *c.* BC	Emergence of an oligarchic state. The functions of the king are taken over by archons, appointed for a year at a time from members of the great families. The Areopagos is established, its membership consisting of former archons.
620 BC	Drakon (Draco) is the first to codify the laws of Attica. The severe penalties provided for in his laws have given us the word "draconic".
594–593 BC	Solon abolishes servitude for debt and gives Athens a new constitution. The population is divided into four groups according to fiscal status. The Council of 400 is established alongside the Areopagos.
560 BC	Peisistratos, a native of Brauron, becomes "tyrant" (sole ruler) of Athens, which enjoys a period of prosperity under his rule. (Dionysiac festivals, drama, black-figured ceramics, etc.)
528–527 BC	Peisistratos dies and is succeeded by his sons Hippias and Hipparchos.
514 BC	Hippias is murdered.
510 BC	Fall of the tyranny: Hipparchos is expelled from Athens.
508–507 BC	Kleisthenes reforms the state; establishment of democracy. The population of Attica is divided into ten tribes (phylai), which appoint 50 members each to the Council of 500. Introduction of ostracism.
490 BC	The Athenians defeat the Persians at Marathon. Thermistokles secures approval of his fleet-building programme.
480 BC	The Persians, under Xerxes, again invade Greece, break through at Thermopylai and devastate Athens and the Acropolis. Athens defeats the Persian fleet at Salamis.
479 BC	Final victory over the Persians (battles of Plataiai Mykale). Building of the Themistoclean Walls.
461 BC	Perikles becomes the dominant figure in Athens: beginning of the "age of Perikles". Building programme on the Acropolis.
445 BC	Perikles concludes a 30 years' armistice with Sparta.
431–404 BC	Peloponnesian war between Athens and Sparta. The war ends in the defeat of Athens (destruction of the Attic fleet at Aigospotamoi). Sparta establishes the rule of the "Thirty Tyrants" in Athens.
429 BC	Death of Perikles.

The Acropolis got its new appearance under Perikles

Sokrates is condemned to death.	399 BC
Establishment of the second Attic Maritime League.	377 BC
Philip II of Macedon establishes his authority over the whole of Greece at the battle of Chaironeia.	338 BC
Philip of Macedon is murdered.	336 BC
Alexander the Great consolidates Macedonian authority in Greece and establishes a world empire.	336–323 BC
Death of Alexander the Great.	323 BC
Large building enterprises by Hellenistic kings of Pergamon and Syria: Stoa of Attalos, Stoa of Eumenes, work on Olympieion.	2nd c. BC
Greece becomes a Roman province.	146 BC
The Apostle Paul preaches in Athens.	AD 50
The Emperor Hadrian founds the "city of Hadrian" around the Olympieion, which he completes.	117–38
The Herulians, an eastern Germanic people, devastate Athens. The "Valerian Wall" is built to protect the much reduced area of the city.	267
The Goths under Alarich enter Athens.	395
A large Gymnasion is built in the Agora to house the University of Athens.	c. 400

Chronology

426	The Christian Emperor of the East, Theodosius II, orders the closing of pagan places of worship. Some of the temples (the Temple of Hephaistos) are converted into churches. The first purpose-built churches are erected.
529	The Emperor Justinian closes Athens University and Plato's Academy.
869	Athens becomes the see of an archbishop.
1085	The Emperor Basil II visits Athens, now no more than a small country town – the only Byzantine emperor to do so.
1203–4	After the fourth Crusade Athens becomes the residence of a Frankish duke, who converts the Propylaia on the Acropolis into his palace.
1311	Catalan mercenaries occupy the town.
1418	Albanians settle in Attica.
1456	Sultan Mehmet II conquers Athens. The Parthenon becomes a mosque. Beginning of the Turkish period.
1668	French Capuchin friars incorporate the Monument of Lysikrates in their convent.
1674	De Mointel, French ambassador in Constantinople, visits Athens and has drawings made of the ancient remains.
1678	A Venetian, Morosini, takes the Acropolis. A Venetian grenade destroys the Parthenon.
1821	The Greek war of independence begins. Athens is taken by rebel Greek forces.
1826	The Turks retake Athens.
1830	The three great powers – Britain, France and Russia – declare Greece to be an independent sovereign kingdom.
1832	The powers recognise the Bavarian prince Otto of Wittelsbach as king of Greece.
1833	The Turks finally leave Athens (12 April). Otto of Bavaria, first king of Greece, arrives.
1834	King Otto I makes Athens capital of Greece.
1843	After a bloodless military rising Greece becomes a constitutional monarchy.
1862	King Otto I is deposed.
1864	The Danish prince William George of Glücksburg is elected king as George I.
1896	The first Modern Olympic Games are held in Athens, with 285 competitors from eleven nations. 43 gold medals are awarded.
1911–13	Balkan Wars. Greece wins Epirus, Macedonia, Crete and Samos.
1913	George I is murdered in Salonica. Succeeded by Constantine.

After the Greek defeat in the war with Turkey, Athens has to take in some 300,000 refugees from Asia Minor. Whole new districts are developed.	1923
George II is deposed. Greece becomes a republic.	1924
Restoration of the monarchy. George II returns to the throne.	1935
Following a *coup d'état* General Metaxas sets up a dictatorship.	1936
Germany invades Greece. A government in exile is set up in London.	1941
Liberation of Athens. Beginning of civil war.	1944
The civil war ends in the defeat of the Communists.	1949
Military putsch: the military government of Papadopoulos comes to power. After an unsuccessful attempt at a counter-putsch King Constantine II leaves Greece.	1967
President Gizikis brings Constantine Karamanlis back from exile as Prime Minister.	1974
New republican constitution.	1975
Greece becomes a member of the European Community. The Socialist Andreas Papandreou becomes head of government.	1981
Papandreou is re-elected prime minister	1985
Peace conference in Piraeus with delegates from NATO, the Warsaw Pact and non-aligned countries. Large demonstrations and strikes in Athens against the Socialist government's economic policies.	1986

The Turkish prime minister Turgut Özal comes to Athens for political discussions.
    The West German president Richard von Weizsäcker makes a state visit to Greece and pays homage to fallen Greek freedom fighters of the Second World War.
    Eleven people are killed in a terrorist attack on the pleasure ship "City of Poros" as it was returning to Athens from the island of Hýdra.
	1988

Papandreou is voted out of office. The "Nea Demokratia" and the Communists form an interim government in an attempt to resolve various bribery scandals.	1989

The Greek Conservative politician Karamanlis is elected president of Greece for the second time.
    In September public services are paralysed by a general strike.
    Serious riots in Athens.
	1990

The Mediterranean Games are held in the new sports arena.	1991
The Pasok, led by Papandréou, wins the parliamentary elections.	1993
Parliament instates the independent Konstantinos Stephanopoulos as the new president.	1995
Papandreous stands sown for health reasons. His successor Konstantinos Simitis secures a place in government for the Pasok by winning a majority in parliamentary elections.	1996
Athens is chosen as the host for the Olympics 2004.	1997

Capital of the Hellenes

When Ottoman troops conquered Athens in 1456, no-one thought that Turkish rule would last until 1830 and that it would take until 1834 before Athens would become the capital of the new Greek state. The Sultan administrated his expansive empire from Constantinople with a minimum of effort using a system of favouritism, encouraging competition and punishing transgression, while spending little time worrying about the welfare of occupied areas. Remarkable, however, was the Ottoman tolerance of religion. The Greek Orthodox Church enjoyed privileges and held both spiritual and at times civil power.

When the central government in Constantinople began to weaken, local rulers behaved in a high-handed manner, and increased their taxes on the peasants. Eventually, around 1800 and spurred on in part by the French revolution, simmering national and social conflicts broke to the surface and encouraged the Greek demand for self-determination. In 1800 the Ionic islands, which until 1797 had belonged to Venice, formed the Republic of the Seven United Islands; and by 1815 they had become a British protectorate. In 1803, the Greek Albanian Suliots rose against Turkish domination, and the Serbs followed a year later. In all cases, the weakness of the Ottoman Empire was apparent, which encouraged the Greeks to rebel too.

Their resistance, however, developed only slowly, organised by such diverse groups as the secret league of the Hetary and the *Klephts* (groups of brigands). The Greek merchants, who through trade had come into contact with the Enlightenment and the culture of western Europe, played an important role in the formation of a national consciousness. The Sultan was well aware of such dangers and had, therefore, tried to head off such rebellions by favouring certain groups of Greeks such as the Phanariots and binding them more closely to the court by promoting them to important administrative posts. The impetus for an uprising against the Ottoman Empire therefore had to come largely from outside the country.

In 1814, under the leadership of Count Alexandros Ypsilanti, Greek merchants formed a secret society in the Russian town of Odessa, to encourage opposition to Turkish rule. In March 1821 finally, Ypsilanti, relying on Russian assistance, invaded the Moldavia region with a small troop and called for national insurrection. As Russian support did not materialise, his undertaking failed at first. But unexpected help arrived in April when Germanos of Pátras called for insurrection: in May 1821 the Greeks with their united troops succeeded in bringing the Peloponnese as well as Athens under their control. After forming a provisional government, the independence of the Hellenic people was declared on 1st January 1822, and a national assembly was convened at Epidauros. At the same time, a wave of sympathy for the Greek freedom fighters swept Europe. In 1824 the British poet Lord Byron arrived in Missolonghi from Italy in order to fight for the Greek cause, only to die shortly after of malaria.

The Turkish counter-offensive mobilised slowly, but scored a success when the Turkish governor of Egypt resubjugated the Peloponnese in 1825–6 and re-occupied Athens in August 1826. In the meantime, the superpowers Russia, England and France supported Greek independence and exerted pressure on the Ottoman

The history of modern Greece is represented in the National Historical Museum

Empire with the Treaty of London. In the Battle of Navarino in 1827, thanks to the intervention of the superpowers, victory over the Turco-Egyptian naval forces was decisive. In the same year, the Greek Count Ioannis Kapodistrias, who had previously been employed in the Russian diplomatic service, was appointed as president by the National Assembly. It is thanks to his diplomatic skills that in the Russo-Turkish peace negotiations and the London Protocol of 1829 the borders of the new Greek state were fixed and the sovereignty of the kingdom of Greece was recognised in 1830 by all the powers concerned.

After the assassination of Kapodistrias in 1831 the superpowers chose the still under-age Prince Otto of Bavaria as contender for the throne in 1832, and in the same year he was confirmed as future king by the National Assembly. The question of a capital was not resolved until 1834 when Athens was chosen as residence for the king. When King Otto took over his official duties in Athens in 1835, he was only poorly accommodated in the provincial town which had descended into complete irrelevance; Athens was in urgent need of reconstruction. But it had no urban bourgeoisie, and the king, too, imbued with a completely outmoded enthusiasm for Greece, ruled in an almost absolutist way and lacked a sense of reality. Despite announcing a constitution in 1844, Otto was not capable of solving even the most pressing economic, political and social problems, so that he was deposed in 1862 and went into exile in Bamberg. Prince William of Denmark followed him onto the throne in 1863 as King George I. Domestically, the situation remained difficult, but instead he notched up some successes abroad. Thus, in 1864 the Ionic Islands were annexed by Greece.

Meanwhile in Athens, the programme begun by King Otto to beautify the residential town in the classicial and historicist style could be continued. The Athenians would have loved to regard their town as the capital of a reborn Byzantine Empire, but this 'big idea' faltered in the political reality, because an agricultural country based on a small-holder structure had no chance to overpower a superpower like the Ottoman Empire. Hence not all of Hellas gained its freedom in the 19th century.

Famous People

Aischylos/ Aeschylus (525–456 BC)

Aeschylus was the founder of tragedy as we know it today: the history of European drama begins with him, for no plays written before his time have been preserved.

The tragedy was originally a "goat-song" (tragos, "goat", odi, "song") in honour of the god Dionysos. Earlier Thespis had put on performances with one actor and a chorus: Aeschylus' great innovation was to have two actors together with the chorus, thus making possible for the first time a dialogue and genuinely dramatic action. The chorus, limited to 12 members, was now reduced to the function of merely commenting on this dialogue. The main theme of the Aeschylean tragedies is the fateful tension between the gods and man, who is doomed to destruction if he rebels against the gods. Of Aeschylus' 90 tragedies five have been preserved complete: the "Persians", "Prometheus", the "Seven against Thebes", the "Suppliant Women" and the "Oresteia", a trilogy consisting of "Agamemnon", the "Libation-Bearers" and the "Eumenides".

Aeschylus was born in Eleusis and fought in the battle of Marathon (490 BC), as his epitaph recorded. After the success of the "Persians" (472 BC) he accepted an invitation from Hieron I, tyrant of Gela and Syracuse, to go to Sicily, but later returned to Athens. After coming into conflict with Pericles, who regarded the "Oresteia" as hostile criticism of himself, Aeschylus withdrew into voluntary exile at Gela.

Anaxagoras (c. 500–428 BC)

The Greek natural philosopher Anaxagoras was born c. 500 BC in Klazomenai near Smyrna (Izmir). He came to Athens as a young man and became very highly thought of there, but was later charged with heresy. He avoided the clutches of the court by fleeing to Lampsakos, on the east bank of the Dardanelles/Hellespont, where he died in 428 BC. Anaxagoras was the first to trace all being back to minute, qualitatively different elements ("spermata"), claiming that they are set in motion by a cosmic and all-powerful reason ("nus") and made into things by the separation of varying or the combination of similar particles. However, only fragments of his writings have been preserved.

Antisthenes (c. 440–360 BC)

Antisthenes was an enthusiastic follower of the philosopher Socrates. Soon after Socrates' death he founded the philosophical school of the Cynics (from kynikos, "dog-like", i.e. with no more needs than a dog). Antisthenes preached a philosophy of deliberate poverty and the reduction of human needs to a minimum. The Cynics were also known as "dog-like" because they fell upon men as dogs do and sought to convert them to their philosophy. From this the word "cynic" has degenerated to its present meaning.

Aristophanes (c. 445–385 BC)

Aristophanes was the leading writer of the Athenian "Old Comedy". Eleven of his 40 plays have been preserved, and some of them, including "Lysistrata", "The Birds", "Peace" and the "Acharnians", are still performed.

Aristotle, a native of Stageira (Macedonia), was a pupil of Plato at the Academy from 367 to 348 BC and thereafter went to Macedonia as tutor to Alexander the Great, returning in 336 to Athens, where he founded a school of philosophy in the Lykeion (Lyceum). His pupils were known as Peripatetics after the *peripatos* (covered walk) of the Lykeion.

Aristoteles/
Aristotle
(384–322 BC)

Out of his numerous works a number of systematic treatises have been preserved, covering logic, the natural sciences, metaphysics, ethics, politics and poetics. "Aristotle sought to study the actual scientific content of phenomena in order to achieve an understanding of their essential substance. He was the creator and organiser of the scientific division of labour." (Buchwald.)

Democritus, a native of Abdera in Thrace, lived in Athens as a philosopher and scientist, developing his Atomist theory. This sophisticated theory anticipated Locke's distinction between primary and secondary qualities.

Demokritos/
Democritus
(c. 460–c. 380 BC)

Demosthenes, the most famous of the Attic orators, inveighed against Philip II and the powerful kingdom of Macedonia. After the deaths of Philip and his son Alexander Demosthenes was condemned to death by Antipater and fled to the island of Kalaureia, where he took poison in the sanctuary of Poseidon in order to escape arrest.

Demosthenes
(384–322 BC)

The poet Odysseas Elytis (real name Alepudelis) was born in Iráklion on Crete. He grew up in Athens where he studied law. He lived in the city until his death.

Odysseas Elytis
(1911–96)

Odysseas Elytis belonged to the circle around Giorgos Seferis who was instrumental in rejuvenating the New Greek poetry in the 1930s. Both were awarded the Nobel Prize for Literature, Seferis in 1963 and Elytis in 1979. Elytis' poems are marked by a pronounced naturalism. His most important work, the cycle of poems "To axion esti" published in 1959, was set to music by Mikis Theodorakis.

The Greek philosopher Epicurus was born on the island of Samos and worked as a teacher first in Mytilene on Lésbos and then in Lamsakos on the left bank of the Dardanelles. In 306 BC he opened his own school in a garden in Athens, known as "The Garden of Epicurus". His philosophy, passed down to us in three large essays and numerous fragments of his writings, is devoted to life on earth, recognising that the happiness of the individual is to be achieved through personal goals and findings, definitions and evidence.

Epikouros/
Epicurus
(341–270 BC)

The work of Epicurus deals with the three great topics of the theory of knowledge based on observation and awareness, physics based on Democrit's teachings of the movement of the atom, and the ethic of repose of the soul and virtue. Epicurus died in Athens in 271 BC.

Epicureanism as put forward later by Zenon and Demetrios met with much approval, but rapidly deteriorated into a banal form of hedonism, the advocacy of unrestrained enjoyment.

The Latin word "epicurus" denoted one preferring sensual pleasure.

Euripides was the founder of the psychological drama, the tragedy of character. He believed, with the sophist Protagoras, that man was the "measure of all things"; and in the tragedies of Euripides it is no longer the gods who sway the fates of men but man himself who lives his own life and destroys himself or wrestles with his own very personal problems.

Euripides
(c. 480–c. 406 BC)

Of his 75 known dramas 19 have been preserved, including "Alcestis" (438), "Medea" (431), the "Children of Heracles" (c. 430), "Andromache" (c. 429), "Hecuba" (c. 425), "Electra" (c. 413), "Heracles" (after 423), the "Trojan Women" (415), "Helena" (412), "Iphigenia in Tauris" (c. 412), "Orestes" (408), "Iphigenia in Aulis" (after 407–406), the "Bacchae" (after 407–406) and a satyric play, "Cyclops".

The plays of Euripides have influenced the whole development of drama in Europe. Almost all his dramas have been re-worked or imitated by later dramatists, from Corneille and Racine to Goethe and Schiller, Franz Grillparzer and Jean-Paul Sartre.

Herodes Atticus
(c. AD 101–177)

Herodes Atticus, a native of Marathon, spent much of his life in Athens, where he was a teacher of rhetoric and held various important public offices. He employed his immense wealth in munificent benefactions, endowing Athens with a temple of Tyche, the Odeion (still preserved) that bears his name, on the S side of the Acropolis, and the marble Stadion (restored in the 19th c.), near which he was buried.

Herodotus
(c. 490–425 BC)

Herodotus, described by Cicero as "The Father of Historical Writings", was born in Halikarnassos (now Bodrum, in south-west Turkey), but was obliged to leave his homeland as a result of his involvement in the uprising against the tyrant Lygdamis. Many long journeys took him to Egypt and Africa, Mesopotamia, the Black Sea coast and Italy. Later he lived in Athens, where he was highly respected, and in 444 BC he settled in the newly-founded Athenian colony at Thurioi (Thurii) in Italy.

Published some time later, his major work was divided into nine books named after the Muses, and concerns itself with both critical and positive assessments of the countries he had visited and of their politics. The highlight is his description of the Persian Wars. More recent documentation has confirmed the reliability of his reports, and Herodotus has provided us not only with an impressive account of his life spent in Asia Minor and Greece, but also valuable ethnographic and geographical records of countries in the Near East and Africa.

Iktinos/Ictinus
(5th c. BC)

Ictinus (place of origin unknown) was the architect of the Parthenon in Athens (449–438 BC), the classical Telesterion at Eleusis and the temple of Apollo at Phigaleia. He established the Attic style of architecture, a combination of Doric and Ionic elements.

Melina Mercouri
(1925–94)

"I was born a Greek" is the title of Melina Mercouri's autobiography, published in 1971. She had just been expatriated by the military Junta because she had been campaigning abroad against the dictatorship of the colonels. When the military took power in the putsch of 1967, Melina Mercouri was already a famous actress and an acclaimed singer of *chansons*. The daughter of a former minister of the interior and granddaughter of the long-standing Mayor of Athens, she had her greatest success with the film "Never on Sundays", directed by her husband, Jules Dassin. In the film, she played the temperamental and warm-hearted

prostitute Ilya, and sang the song, "A ship is coming" which became a popular hit. After her return from exile she continued to be actively involved in politics. As Minister for Cultural Affairs for two parliamentary terms (1981–89) in the PASOK government, she unsuccessfully demanded of the British government the return of the "Elgin Marbles", decorative parts from the Acropolis temple complex which Lord Elgin had taken to London after 1799.

Otto I, son of King Ludwig I of Bavaria, was the first king of Greece (1833–62). He ruled at first with a Regency council because of his young age, and later as an absolute monarch, but in 1843 was compelled to grant a constitution.

Otto I
(1815–67)

He promoted the building of the modern city of Athens and the development of Greece into a European state.

He was deposed in 1862 largely due to his inability to tackle the most pressing economic and social problems. He was exiled to Germany, where he died. He and his queen, Amalia, are buried in Munich.

Andreas Papandréou simultaneously embodied Greece's new-found national self-confidence after the colonels' dictatorship and old-style high-handedness. The son of the politician Georgios Papandréou, his life underwent many changes before he became the formative politician of the 1980s. Even as a student at the Faculty of Law and Economics at Athens University, he was already opposed to the dictatorship of General Metaxás. He was arrested in 1939 and emigrated to the United States in the following year where he taught at various universities until 1960. From 1964 to 1967 he was a member of the Greek parliament, and in 1965 he became a minister in his father's Cabinet. After a

Andreas
Papandréou
(1919–96)

second period in exile during the military dictatorship, Papandréou founded the Panhellenic Socialist Movement (PASOK) and won a clear majority in the 1981 parliamentary elections. Plagued by scandals and accusations of corruption, Papandréou had to resign his office as President in 1989. In 1992, however, he was cleared of all accusations and again helped PASOK to gain the majority in the 1993 parliamentary elections.

Pericles, Athens' greatest statesman, gave his name to the city's glorious heyday, the "age of Pericles".

Perikles/Pericles
(c. 495–429 BC)

In 472 BC he was choregos ("leader" of the choris, who met its expenses) in a performance of Aeschylus' "Persians". In 461 he became leader of the democratic party, and in 443 the sole ruler and elected military leader of Athens.

Famous People

In 454 he transferred the treasury to the Attic League from the island of Delos to Athens and used it to finance the constructions of the new buildings on the Acropolis, which was now given its classical form.

With his mistress Aspasia, he promoted the arts and sciences, and was a friend of the sculptor Phidias, the philosopher Anaxagoras and the dramatist Sophocles. In 431 he was responsible for the outbreak of the Peloponnesian War. He died of plague in 429.

Pheidias/Phidias
(5th c. BC)

Phidias was recognised in ancient times as the greatest sculptor of the classical period of Athens. He was entrusted by Pericles with the general direction of the great building programme on the Acropolis, for which he created the bronze statue of Athena Promachos and the chryselephantine (gold and ivory) statue of Athena Parthenos in the Parthenon. He was also responsible for some of the architectural sculpture on the Parthenon. No less renowned than the Athena Parthenos was his chryselephantine seated figure of Zeus at Olympia. In 432–431 BC he was accused of misappropriating gold intended for the statue of Athena, and is believed to have died in prison.

Platon/Plato
(c. 427–c. 347 BC)

Plato, the greatest philosopher of ancient Greece, was a native of Athens and a scion of the Attic nobility. He was a pupil of Socrates for eight years, until his master's death in 399 BC. After travelling in Sicily he returned to Athens and in 387 founded his school, the Academy, in form a cultic association but in practice a place of philosophical study. The central feature of Plato's philosophy is the theory of ideas. His works, 36 in number, are preserved complete. With the exception of the "Apology of Socrates" they are all in dialogue form.

Praxiteles
(4th c. BC)

Praxiteles, who ranked with Scopas and Lysippus as one of the leading sculptors of his day, came of a family of Athenian sculptors and was a pupil of his father Cephisodotus. He worked mainly in marble but also produced work in bronze. Particularly famous in antiquity were his Aphrodite of Cnidos, Hermes with the boy Dionysos at Olympia, Apollo Sauroctonus (the lizard-slayer) and a wounded Amazon – masterpieces of the post-classical style.

Heinrich Schliemann
(1822–90)

Heinrich Schliemann was born in Mecklenburg and began his working life in a commercial business in Amsterdam. In 1847 he established his own business in St Petersburg and made a large fortune. After extensive travels he took up the study of archaeology in Paris in 1866.

Schliemann discovered Troy, Mycenae and other Mycenaean sites, and in 1879 took up residence with his Greek wife Sophia in Athens, in a palatial mansion built for him by Ernst Ziller.

Schliemann died in Naples in 1890 and was buried in the principal cemetery of Athens.

Sokrates/Socrates
(c. 470–c. 399 BC)

Socrates, an Athenian of the deme of Alopece, was married late in life to Xanthippe, who acquired a legendary reputation as a shrew. In 406 BC, as a prytanis (member of a committee of the Council) he defended the rule of law against the will of the popular assembly, and achieved prominence as a philosopher questing for truth in discussion in the Agora and in groups of friends. He never wrote down his teachings, which we know only from the works of his pupils, in particular Plato. In 399 he was condemned to death by drinking hemlock for the corruption of youth. He refused to seek safety in flight and died in the state prison in the Agora, surrounded by his pupils.

The Athenian statesman and poet Solon was later ranked among the Seven Sages of antiquity. As archon (the highest official of Athens) in 594 BC he forbade borrowing on the security of the borrower's person and abolished serfdom. He gave Athens a constitution, laid down the rights of the Areopagos and reformed the currency and the weights and measures of Athens. Then, after making the Athenians swear not to alter his constitution during his absence, he travelled extensively in Egypt and elsewhere.

Solon
(*c.* 640–560 BC)

Sophocles was the second of the great Attic tragic dramatists, coming after Aeschylus and before Euripides. He introduced a third actor (see Aeschylus) and reduced the role of the chorus still further, thus making possible the representation of real characters. It was left to Euripides, however to achieve the psychological representation of character, for in Sophocles man is not yet the "measure of all things" but is still subject to the authority of all-powerful gods. Caught in the bonds of fate, man must struggle and suffer until at last, after this process of "learning through suffering", the smallness and impotence of man in face of the gods is made manifest.

Sophokles/
Sophocles
(*c.* 496–*c.* 406 BC)

Three of the seven dramas by Sophocles that have survived are concerned with the myth of Oedipus – "Oedipus the King", "Oedipus at Colonus" and "'Antigone". His other plays are "Ajax", the "Trachinian Women", "Electra" and "Philoctetes".

The Attic statesman Themistocles, archon in 493, initiated the development of Piraeus into a fortified port, and in 483 persuaded the Athenians to use the profits of the Laurion silver mines for the construction of warships, thus making possible the defeat of the Persian fleet at Salamis in 480. In 479 he fortified Athens. In 474, however, he was "ostracised" and expelled from Athens, and later committed suicide at Magnesia (Asia Minor), which was presented to him by the Persians.

Themistokles/
Themistocles
(*c.* 525–462 BC)

The Greek composer and singer Mikis Theodorakis studied in Athens and Paris under Messiaen. A Member of Parliament for the United Democratic Left from 1963 to 1967, he was imprisoned for three years after the 1967 putsch. Living in exile in Paris from 1970 to 1974, Theodorakis enlisted support for the democratic movement in his country at numerous political solidarity events all over Europe. In 1974 he returned to Greece, and in the 1980s he continued his work as a Member of Parliament. His musical work, which strongly borrows from Greek folk music, is marked by his political involvement.

Mikis Theodorakis
(b. 1925)

Amongst other works, Theodorakis composed orchestral pieces, ballets, theatre and film soundtracks, songs and oratorios (for example "Canto general", a cycle of poems by Pablo Neruda, set to music and completed in 1973).

Thucydides, founder of the science of history, came of a noble family. His "History of the Peloponnesian War", begun immediately after the outbreak of war (431 BC), describes and interprets the course of the conflict down to 411–410 BC. Characteristic features of his work are his concern to achieve objectivity (in spite of his leaning towards the Athenian side), and an understanding of the events of the war through study of the circumstances of the events themselves.

Thoukydides/
Thucydides
(*c.* 460-*c.* 400 BC)

Architecture

Greek Temple

The temple, together with the theatre, is the most characteristic achievement of ancient Greek architecture. It is conceived not as a place of assembly for the faithful but as a shrine housing the cult image of the divinity. Its form is derived from the megaron, the principal room in a Mycenaean palace or house.

Temple in antis

The simplest form is the temple in antis, in which the naos is preceded by an antechamber (the pronaos) flanked by antae (forward projections of the side walls of the naos). Between the antae are two columns supporting the pediment (Treasury of the Athenians, Delphi). A temple with a second antechamber at the far end is known as a double anta temple (temple of Aphaia, Aegina).

Prostyle

Where there is another row of columns in front of the antae, supporting the projecting pediment (one column in front of each of the antae, with two or four between), the temple is known as prostyle (eastern temple in the Erechtheion, Athens).

Amphiprostyle

If there is a similar row of columns on the rear end of the temple it is known as amphiprostyle (Temple of Nike, Acropolis, Athens).

Peripteral

From the second half of the 7th century the classical form was the peripteral temple, in which the naos was surrounded on all four sides by

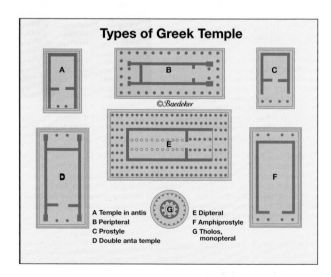

Types of Greek Temple

©Baedeker

A Temple in antis
B Peripteral
C Prostyle
D Double anta temple
E Dipteral
F Amphiprostyle
G Tholos, monopteral

a colonnade (peristasis). At one end was the entrance, with the pronaos; at the other end was a rear chamber, the opisthodomos. In the 6th century an elongated ground-plan was favoured, with six columns at the ends and 16 along the sides (temple of Hera, Olympia; temple of Apollo, Delphi, with 6 + 15 columns). In the 5th century the classical proportions of the temple were developed, with the columns along the sides numbering one more than twice the number at the ends (Temple of Zeus, Olympia, 6 + 13 columns; Parthenon, Athens, 8 + 17).

If the temple has a double row of columns on all four sides it is known as dipteral (Olympieion, Athens). If the inner row of columns is omitted to leave room for a wider naos, the temple is known as pseudo-dipteral.

Dipteral
Pseudo-dipteral

A less common type of temple is the tholos, on a circular ground-plan, with a ring of columns round the naos. Examples of this type can be seen at Delphi (Marmaria) and Epidauros.

Tholos

Classical Orders

In the Doric order the shaft of the column, which tapers towards the top and has between 16 and 20 flutings, stands directly, without a base, on the stylobate above the three-stepped crepidoma or platform. A characteristic feature is the entasis (swelling) of the columns, which together with the frequently applied curvature of the crepidoma relieves the austerity of the structure.

Doric order

The capital consists of the echinus, curving up from the shaft, and the square abacus. It carries the architrave with its frieze of triglyphs and metopes, which may be either plain or with relief ornament. Between and below the triglyphs are the drop-like guttae. The tympanon is enclosed by the horizontal cornice (geison) and the oblique mouldings that form an angle with it, and usually contains the pediment figures. The sculptured decoration normally consists of the carving on the metopes and the pediment figures, but may extend also to the front of the pronaos.

Where limestone rather than marble was used it was faced with a coat of stucco. The surface was not left in its natural colour but was painted, the dominant colours being blue, red and white.

The Ionic order has slenderer and gentler forms than the Doric, the "male" order. The flutings of the columns are separated by narrow ridges. The column stands on a base, which may be either of the Anatolian type (with several concave mouldings) or the Attic type (with an alternation between the convex torus and the concave trochilus). The characteristic feature of the capital is the spiral volute (scroll) on either side. The architrave is not straight, but made up of three sections, each projecting over the one below. The frieze is continuous, without triglyphs to divide it up.

Ionic order

The Ionic type of temple, which originated in the territories occupied by the Ionian Greeks, was well adapted to the development of large structures, such as the gigantic temples on Samos and at Ephesus, Sardis and Didyma in Asia Minor.

The Corinthian order is similar to the Ionic except in the form of the capital.

Corinthian order

The characteristic feature of the Corinthian capital is the acanthus foliage that encloses the circular body of the capital, with tendrils reaching up to the concave architrave (the "master capital" in Epidauros Museum; Olympieion, Athens).

The Corinthian capital was particularly popular in the Imperial period, which also evolved the "composite" capital, a marriage of the Ionic and

Composite capital

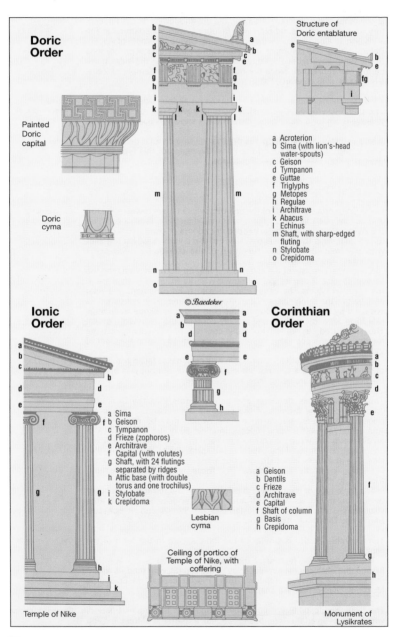

Doric Order

Painted Doric capital

Doric cyma

Structure of Doric entablature

a Acroterion
b Sima (with lion's-head water-spouts)
c Geison
d Tympanon
e Guttae
f Triglyphs
g Metopes
h Regulae
i Architrave
k Abacus
l Echinus
m Shaft, with sharp-edged fluting
n Stylobate
o Crepidoma

©Baedeker

Ionic Order

a Sima
b Geison
c Tympanon
d Frieze (zophoros)
e Architrave
f Capital (with volutes)
g Shaft, with 24 flutings separated by ridges
h Attic base (with double torus and one trochilus)
i Stylobate
k Crepidoma

Lesbian cyma

Ceiling of portico of Temple of Nike, with coffering

Temple of Nike

Corinthian Order

a Geison
b Dentils
c Frieze
d Architrave
e Capital
f Shaft of column
g Basis
h Crepidoma

Monument of Lysikrates

Corinthian forms, and developed ever more elaborate decorative schemes.

Greek Church

When Christian worship was officially permitted in the 4th century the first churches began to be built.

The predominant form was the basilica, with a nave flanked by one or two lower lateral aisles and the altar in an apse at the east end. The entrance was at the west end, with a narthex (porch) preceding the nave, and frequently with an atrium outside the entrance.

Basilica

This type is found throughout the Roman world, from Rome to Jerusalem.

In the 9th century a new type of church developed in Greece, based on a centralised rather than a longitudinal plan. This was the domed cruciform church, which thereafter became predominant.

Domed cruciform church

The central dome is supported either on sections of wall or on columns, occasionally on two sections of wall and two columns. It may span either the nave alone (as at Kaisarianí) or – with eight supports – the nave and aisles (as at Dafni).

The chancel, with the altar, was originally separated from the body of the church by a low stone screen, which later developed into the iconostasis. It is flanked by two small rooms, the prothesis and diakonikon, which serve liturgical purposes; and, matching this tripartite structure, the church usually has three apses. At the west end of the church there is often an exonarthex (outer narthex) preceding the narthex.

The wall and dome paintings in the interior of the church reflect the heavenly hierarchy, with Christ at the highest point of the dome and the Mother of God (the Virgin), patriarchs, prophets and saints at lower levels. The exterior walls are in stone and brick, often elaborately patterned.

In post-Byzantine times there was sometimes a reversion to the old basilican type of church, usually small, with one to three aisles.

Athens in Quotations

Herodotus
Greek historian
(c. 490–c. 425 BC)

On this Acropolis there is a temple of Erechtheus, the Earth-Born, as he is called, and within its precinct are an olive-tree and a pool containing sea-water. The Athenians say that these were put there by Athena and Poseidon during their contest for the land of Attica in token of their taking possession of the land. The olive-tree, however, met the same fate as the rest of the sanctuary: it was burned down by the barbarians. But when on the day after the fire some Athenians went up to the sanctuary to perform a sacrifice at the behest of the Persian king they saw a shoot which had sprung from the stump of a tree to the height of a cubit. And of this they spread the report in the city.

Thucydides
Greek historian
(c. 460–c. 400 BC)

Our constitution does not copy the laws of neighbouring states; we are rather a pattern to others than imitators ourselves. Its administration favours the many instead of the few; this is why it is called a democracy ...

We provide plenty of means for the mind to refresh itself from business. We celebrate games and sacrifice all the year round, and the elegance of our private establishments forms a daily source of pleasure and helps to banish the spleen ...

At Athens we live exactly as we please, and yet are just as ready to encounter every legitimate danger ... and we have the double advantage of escaping the experience of hardships in anticipation and of facing them in the hour of need as fearlessly as those who are never free from them.

Nor are these the only points in which our city is worthy of admiration. We cultivate refinement without extravagance and knowledge without effeminacy; wealth we employ more for use than for show, and place the real disgrace of poverty not in owning to the fact but in declining the struggle against it ...

In short, I say that as a city we are the school of Hellas; while I doubt if the world can produce a man, who where he had only himself to depend upon, is equal to so many emergencies, and graced by so happy a versatility as the Athenian.

From the Funeral Oration of Perikles (Crawley translation)

Isokrates
Greek orator
(436–338 BC)

So far has our city surpassed the rest of mankind in the field of thinking and speaking that her pupils have become the teachers of other men. So much is this so that the name of Hellenes no longer appears to betoken a particular race, but rather a disposition of mind, and is applied to those who share our culture rather than those who share our descent.

"Panegyrikos"

Xenophon
Greek writer
(c. 430–c. 355 BC)

There is excellent foundation for the belief that the city lies approximately in the centre of Greece. For the farther one goes from Athens the more trying does the cold or the heat become; and a man travelling from one end of Greece to the other must pass by way of Athens, as the point at the centre of a circle.

"Ways and Means", 6

The city is very dry and has a poor water supply. The streets are irregular, since the city is so old. At first sight strangers may doubt whether this is indeed the famous city of the Athenians; but they will soon come to believe that it is. For here they will see the fairest things in the world. The theatre is large, imposing and beautiful. The temple of Athena is magnificent, raised high above the world and of great beauty: one is seized with amazement at sight of it. It stands above the theatre and is known as the Parthenon. The Olympieion is only half finished, but the plan of the building makes a profound impression: were it completed it would be a most splendid structure. There are three gymnasia: the Academy, the Lykeion and the Gymnasion of Kynosarges, all set amid trees and lawns. Here too there are all kinds of festivals, entertainment and edification from the philosophers, a variety of pastimes and regular dramatic performances.

Fragments

Herakleides
Greek philosopher
(c. 388–c. 310 BC)

There is no end to it in this city: wherever you set your foot, you encounter some memory of the past.

Cicero
Roman writer
(106–43 BC)

That which was the chief delight of the Athenians and the wonder of strangers, and which alone serves for a proof that the boasted power and opulence of ancient Greece is not an idle tale, was the magnificence of the temples and public edifices. Yet no part of the conduct of Pericles moved the spleen of his enemies more than this ...

Plutarch
Greek philosopher
and historian
(c. AD 50–c. 125)

Pericles answered ... that as the state was provided with all the necessaries of war, its superfluous wealth should be laid out on such works as, when executed, would be eternal monuments of its glory, and which, during their execution, would diffuse a universal plenty; for as so many kinds of labour, and such a variety of instruments and materials were requisite to these undertakings, every art would be exerted, every hand employed, almost the whole city would be in pay, and be at the same time both adorned and supported by itself ...

Thus works were raised of an astonishing magnitude, and inimitable beauty and perfection, every architect striving to surpass magnificence of the design with the elegance of the execution; yet still the most wonderful circumstance was the expedition with which they were completed. Many edifices, each of which seems to have required the labour of several successive ages, were finished during the administration of one prosperous man ...

Hence we have the more reason to wonder, that the structures raised by Pericles should be built in so short a time, and yet built for ages: for as each of them, as soon as finished, had the venerable air of antiquity, so, now they are old, they have the freshness of a modern building.

Langhorne translation

Now while Paul waited for them at Athens, his spirit was stirred in him, when he saw the city wholly given to idolatry. Therefore disputed he in the synagogue with the Jews, and with the devout persons, and in the market daily with them that met with him. Then certain philosophers of the Epicureans, and of the Stoicks, encountered him. And some said, What will this babbler say? other some, He seemeth to be a setter forth of strange gods: because he preached unto them Jesus, and the resurrection. And they took him, and bought him unto Areopagus, saying, May we know what this new doctrine, whereof thou speakest, is? For thou bringest certain strange things to our ears: we would know therefore what these things mean". (For all the Athenians and strangers that were there spent their time in nothing else, but either to tell, or to hear some new thing.)

Then Paul stood in the middle of Mars' hill, and said, Ye men of Athens, I perceive that in all things ye are too superstitious. For as I passed by, and beheld your devotions, I found an altar with this inscription, 'To the unknown God'. Whom therefore ye ignorantly worship, him declare I unto you ...

Howbeit certain men clave unto him, and believed: among the which was Dionysius the Areopagite, and a woman named Damaris, and others with them.

Acts of the Apostles 17, 16–23 and 34

Aelius Aristides
Greek sophist
(c. 117–c. 187)

The inhabitants of this country have on every occasion given splendid and most admirable examples of their disposition, now displaying in the mildness of their manners and in their social intercourse what can truly be called humanity (and no others can aspire to equal them in goodness), now in times of danger and difficulty facing up to the enemy as champions of Greece. And indeed, when we consider the land and the sea, the form of Attica is calculated to bring this about. For it lies in front of Greece like a bulwark, extending eastwards in a peninsula to assert the advanced position that has been assigned to it. It is easy to believe that it was created by the gods for the protection of Hellas, and that it alone was destined by nature to stand at the head of the Greek world.

"Panathenaikos", 95–7

Synesios of
Kyrene
Greek philosopher
(c. AD 370–c. 412)

Accursed be the shipmaster who brought me here! For present-day Athens has nothing left to claim our admiration except its famous name. And just as after a sacrificial animal has been consumed, nothing remains to remind us of it but its skin, so now in this Athens from which philosophy has fled we can but go about the town and admire, perhaps, the Academy and the Lykeion and the Painted Stoa that gave its name to the philosophy of Chrysippos, though the stoa has lost its paintings ... Nowadays it is Egypt that takes up and nurtures the philosophical seed of Hypatia, while Athens, once the haunt of the wise, now appeals only to beekeepers."

Epistula 135

François-René de
Chauteaubriand
French writer
(1768–1848)

From the summit of the Acropolis I watched the sun rise between the two peaks of Mount Hymettos. The crows that nest round the citadel but never fly over it floated in the air below us, their brilliant black wings tinged with pink by the first light of dawn. Columns of light bluish vapour rose from the shadows on the flanks of Hymettos, signalling the presence of gardens and beehives. Athens, the Acropolis and the ruins of the Parthenon were bathed in a delicate peach-blossom hue. The sculptures of Phidias, caught in a horizontal beam of golden light, came to life and seemed to be moving, thanks to the changing play of light and shadow on the contours of the marble.

"Itenéraire de Paris à Jérusalem"

Prince Hermann
von Pückler-
Muskau
German writer
(1785–1871)

A curse condemning them to be ridiculous seems to have been pronounced on the buildings of modern Athens, both public and private. Thus the Ministry of War and Marine has all the appearance of a warehouse, while the royal stables (let us hope a purely temporary structure) reminded me of the establishment of a Berlin bricklayer who has made his pile ...

But in excavating foundations for these houses of cards the workmen smash to pieces the most magnificent old marble pavements and the other ancient remains of which the soil of Athens is so full. It is a real misfortune that the new city is being built on the same site as the ancient one; for this will bury for ever immense treasures of which we know nothing. It is true that the government has ordered that a small open space should be left round each of the monuments that are still standing; but apart from the fact that the government's orders are not universally respected, this does not go nearly far enough.

It may be hoped, however, that at least the king's new palace, lying outside the town at the foot of Lycabettus (where once stood the school of the Cynics), will prove an honourable exception.

Few houses in the town, and few of the trees in the many gardens once found here, have been spared: the Turks are masters in the art of destruction. But the town is rising again with remarkable speed; and though there may be reason to be satisfied with the quantity of the houses the same cannot be said of their quality. Athens has now a very strange aspect: Europeans from every country in the continent, Germans of almost every race and Bavarians of all sorts and conditions rub shoulders with Americans, Turks, Moors and the Greeks themselves; and to all this are added the camels and the palms (of which some few have survived). In Hermes Street, which is the main street – though without a suspicion of paving, rough and rutted, worse than a country lane – you find an inn with a signboard in Greek, German and French, shops belonging to Frank and Bernau of Munich – and now you find me, lodging with my son. This may make you feel at home; but yet it is a strange world of its own, with the ruins left by both Greek and Romans.

King Ludwig I of
Bavaria
(1786–1868)

Extract from a letter to Eduard von Schenck

**Sights
from A to Z**

Sights from A to Z

Suggestions on how to plan a short stay in Athens will be found under Sightseeing in the Practical Information section.

Museums

As the opening times of museums in Greece often change, it is not possible to ensure that the current times are always shown in the guide. It is advisable, therefore, before making a visit to check the times; if necessary by contacting the Greek Tourist Agency EOT. Most museums close on Monday.

Academy of Plato   J/K 6

Location
Kímonos Street
W of railway
station

Bus
051

The Academy (**Akademía Plátonos**) – probably named after the hero Hekademos, who had a cult grove here – lay 1.5 km (1 mi.) north-west of the Dipylon (a double fortified gateway with two inner and two outer towers, see Kerameikos), with which it was linked by a road 40 m (130 ft) wide. From 387 BC onwards this was the meeting-place of Plato and his pupils, the first academy in the world.

Excavations in this outlying district of Athens, beyond the railway line, have revealed remains of a square hall (between Efklídou and Tripóleos streets), immediately north of this a small temple which may have been dedicated to the hero Hekademos, and a large complex of the Roman imperial period built round an inner courtyard.

Bronze Age site

Here, too, was found a structure measuring 8.5 by 4.5 m (28 by 15 ft) now roofed over, the oldest building so far discovered in Athens, dating from the Early Bronze Age (2300–2100 BC).

Kolonós Hippios

From the area of the Academy Tripóleos Street turns north-west to the nearby hill of Kolonós Hippios, which gave its name to the deme (district) of Kolonos, home of the great dramatist Sophocles (496–406 BC) and the setting of his play "Oedipus on Kolonos", written at the age of 90. The hill is now surrounded by a rather poor quarter of Athens. On it are tombstones commemorating two 19th c. archaeologists, Carl Otfried Müller (1797–1840) and François Lenormant (1837–83).

Achárnes

Excursion
12 km (7½ mi.) N

Buses
from Omónia
Square

This site of Achárnes was occupied from Mycenaean times, and in the classical period, as Acharnai, it was a place of some consequence. It is the setting of Aristophanes' comedy "The Acharnians". The village (pop. 3000) is reached from Omónia Square by way of Vathis Square and Liossion Street.

3 km (2 mi.) south of Achárnes, on the west side of the road, is a Mycenaean tholos tomb. The ancient acropolis was on a hill to the W.

★★Acropolis   L 7/8

Location
City centre

A great crag of limestone rising out of the plain of Attica offered a site well adapted for the Acropolis, the fortified citadel of Athens. At first it served both as the stronghold of the kings of Athens and as the site of the city's oldest shrines; later it was reserved for the service of the divinities of Athens alone. This religious centre of ancient Athens, which received its classical form in the time of Pericles, thus reflected the humane values of Greek culture and thought which have retained their power down to our own day. In spite of the destruction wrought by many centuries, most notably the devastating explosion in 1687, when a Venetian grenade blew up a Turkish powder magazine which had been housed in the Parthenon and made the 2000-year-old temple a ruin, the surviving remains still convey something of the splendour of the age of Pericles.

During the 19th and early 20th c. the removal of post-classical structures and extensive works of restoration revealed the remains of the classical buildings of the 5th c. BC. This process began in 1836, immediately after the liberation from Turkish rule, with the restoration (by Ludwig Ross, a German archaeologist on King Otto's staff) of the temple of Athena Nike, which had been incorporated in a Turkish bastion, and culminated in the re-erection of the columns on the north side of the Parthenon in the 1920s.

But the 20th c. has also contrived to wreak more destruction than the Acropolis had suffered in the preceding two and half millennia. The fumes and pollution created by the swarming population and constant traffic of a great modern city, the damage caused by the landing and taking off of aircraft (which are now forbidden to overfly the Acropolis), and the three million visitors who climb up to the Acropolis every year have worn down the surface of the rock and the marble facing of the monuments, while the marble itself has suffered chemical change and the surviving classical sculpture (e.g. on the west frieze of the Parthenon) is flaking away – all this at an alarming pace and on a disturbing scale.

Accordingly UNESCO set up a 15-million-dollar programme to save the Acropolis. The first steps have been to lay a wooden gangway through the Propylaia and to exclude the public from the structures flanking the Propylaia and the interior of the Parthenon. The caryatids have been removed from the Erechtheion – swathed during this process

Electric Railway
Theseion station

Bus
230

Open Mon.–Fri.
8am–6.30pm, Sat.,
Sun., pub. hols
8am–2.30pm

Admission fee

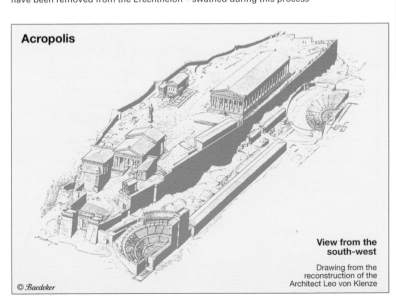

Acropolis

View from the south-west

Drawing from the reconstruction of the Architect Leo von Klenze

© Baedeker

in scaffolding – and placed in the Acropolis Museum, where they can be protected from further damage.

How far the measures already taken and the others which are planned will contribute to the preservation of this incomparable monument of antiquity is, however, still an open question.

History The Acropolis crag measures 320 m (1050 ft) from east to west and 156 m (512 ft) from north to south and rises to 156 m (512 ft) at its highest point. It falls steeply down on the north, east and south, so that since the earliest times the only access has been from the west.

In the Mycenaean period the "cyclopean" walls around the citadel closely followed the contours of the crag. In the north wall were two small gates leading down to the Klepsydra spring and the caves on the north face of the rock. The site of the later Old Temple of Athena was occupied by a royal palace, and there were dwelling houses to the east of the Erechtheion.

The Archaic period (7th and 6th c. BC) is represented by the remains of some ten buildings and parts of two temples.

All the buildings of the Archaic period were destroyed by the Persians in 480 BC. During the reconstruction, which was begun immediately afterwards, Themistocles re-used column drums and fragments of entablature from the destroyed buildings, still to be seen in the north wall. Later, after 467 BC, the south side of the defences was altered by Kimon, who built the straight length of wall which still exists. Inside the Themistoclean north wall and Kimon's south wall the ground surface was built up, using the remains of buildings and sculpture which had been destroyed or damaged by the Persians. In this "Persian rubble" excavations in 1885–6 brought to light numerous pieces of sculpture and

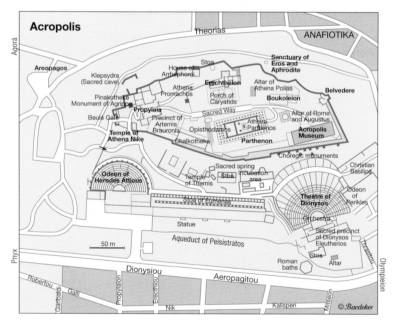

architectural fragments which are now among the treasures of the Acropolis Museum.

Within the extended area of Kimon's stronghold Pericles carried out his great programme of building and rebuilding:

447–438 BC the Parthenon;

437–432 BC the Propylaia;

432–421 BC the temple of Athena Nike;

421–406 BC the Erechtheion.

The only remains dating from a later period are those of a circular temple dedicated to Rome and Augustus (early Imperial period) outside the east end of the Parthenon.

The Acropolis is entered by the Beulç Gate (named after the 19th c. French archaeologist who discovered it), below the west side of the Propylaia, which was the real entrance; admission tickets are sold here. The gate was built in 280 BC of material from the monument of Nikias and other structures. With its two flanking towers, it lay on the axis of symmetry of the Propylaia, with which it was linked by a broad marble staircase built in the reign of the Emperor Septimius Severus; part of the lower section of the staircase still survives.

Beulé Gate

The Klepsydra spring, which, from the earliest times, supplied the Acropolis with water is at the west end of the northern face of the Acropolis. A rock-cut staircase beginning at the Beulé Gate, now walled up, gave access to the spring, which lies below the caves of Apollo and Pan. A well-house was built after the Persian wars.

Klepsydra

On the way up from the Beulé Gate to the Propylaia, immediately below the Pinakotheke, is the tall rectangular plinth, in two colours of marble, of a monument built in the 2nd c. BC for a benefactor of Athens, perhaps a king of Pergamon. It is named after Marcus Agrippa, Augustus's son-in-law, whose quadriga (four-horse chariot) was set up on the base in 27 BC.

Agrippa Monument

The Propylaia were built by Mnesikles in 437–432 BC as a monumental tripartite entrance to the Acropolis, taking the place of a 6th c. propylon of which traces can still be seen. On the native rock is set a flight of marble steps, the lowest step of grey Eleusinian marble, the others of light-coloured Pentelic marble. The central part of the structure is a vestibule with a rear wall containing five gateways, which increase in width and height from the sides to the centre. The lintel of the central doorway has an additional metope – a solution adopted here for the first time which later became common.

★Propylaia

To the west is a deep portico, with a central doorway framed in Ionic columns. Along the front of this portico are six Doric columns that originally supported the pediment. Compared with this imposing entrance the east portico, also with Doric columns but shorter and lower, appears small and modest when seen from the higher part of the Acropolis, subordinating itself to the more important cult buildings. Adjoining the west portico are other structures, including the Pinakotheke, which contained a collection of paintings. To the west of this is a plinth of the 2nd c. BC which was later occupied by a monument to Agrippa.

On the south side a building similar to the Pinakotheke was planned, but this bold plan had to be modified to take account of the old sanctuary of Athena Nike, and in Mnesikles' hands it became merely a narrow vestibule leading to the temple of Nike.

From the 13th c. onwards the Propylaia served as the residence of rulers and military commanders and as defensive fortifications, and were much altered and disfigured. The holes which supported beams bearing intermediate floors can still be seen. The central structure was destroyed between 1640 and 1656 by the explosion of an ammunition

Culture, Art and Politics

The Acropolis, the ancient centre of the arts, and the Agora, the ancient place for trade and political decisions, both dominate the skyline of Athens, even as ruins. The Acropolis, once called the High or Upper Town and the location of the king's fortress, was turned into the present large temple structure and the sole place of worship for the town's goddess Athena by the tyrant Peisistratos. Her support, after all, had helped the Athenians to be victorious in the battle with the Persians, although they had to suffer the destruction of their town in the process. In gratitude, during the long reign of the statesman Pericles between 448/447 and 438/437 BC, the architects Iktinos and Kallikrates were asked to erect the monumental Parthenon Temple by the citizens of Athens. In addition, under the overall direction of the sculptor Phidias, grandiose sculptural decorations were created between 438 and 433 BC, with the 92 metope plates representing the great mythical battles, and the approximately 50 gable figures depicting the birth of Athena in the western gable and her fight with Poseidon for Attica in the eastern gable. After a remarkably brief construction period of only 15 years, the masterpiece, the Athena Parthenos Temple dedicated to the town's goddess, was completed in 432 BC.

The enormous costs for the redesign of the Acropolis, however, had to be borne not by the Athenians themselves, but by their confederates. Thanks to their naval forces who, in 480 BC, were victorious at sea against the Persians, the Athenians had become the predominant sea power of the Attic League, and forced their confederates to pay tribute, even after the Persian peril had been banished. Athens subjugated those who tried to stop payments, such as the town of Chalkis. The money that was collected from the members of the federation was used to finance the urban regeneration programme, especially the re-building of the Acropolis, without any accountability. The reconstruction of the Acropolis, and especially of the Parthenon Temple were at the same time a giant job creation scheme and served the Athenian desire for self-representation. No effort or costs were spared for the most famous piece in the Parthenon, the 12-metre high gold and ivory statue of the goddess, created by Phidias. All visible body parts consisted of ivory while her garments were made from detachable gold plates. A richly adorned helmet topped by a sphinx and framed by winged horses and cheek plates decorated with griffins adorned Athena's head. In her right hand, the goddess held a winged Nike, in her bent arm a lance with gilded tip. Her left hand loosely rested on the shield that had a serpent coiled around its inner rim, while on the inside it showed a gorgon's head and on the outside it was decorated with a gigantomachy which represented the battle between the Athenians and the Amazons.

Around the temple's cell ran a relief frieze, 160 metres long and 10 metres high, with a remarkable impression of depth, depicting the Pan-Athenian festival procession. Here the citizens of Athens portrayed themselves, with over 360 people and more than 200 horses. Every four years, for the birthday celebrations of the town's goddess, this procession went from the Dipylon Gate via the Agorá up to the Acropolis, to witness the ceremonial donation of a peplos, especially woven by Attic virgins for the goddess' statue. Athenians had a lot to thank their patron goddess for, after all, for she had brought wealth to Attica by planting the first olive tree. She was also credited with numerous inventions such as the plough, the rake, the oxen's yoke, the horse's bridle, the potter's firing oven, ships and chariots. She had taught women how to cook, spin and weave. And as a special gift, Athena possessed wisdom, symbolised by the owl.

Guarded by the goddess, the residential and business quarter called Asty stretched along the foot of the Acropolis, with its modest houses built up around the monumental Agorá, the site of democracy, the Athenian rule of the people. The political structures had only slowly evolved from monarchy via an oligarchy of the aristocracy through the subsequent period of tyranny and up to democracy, which was perfected in the 5th century BC under the statesman Pericles. Athenians

Parthenon: detail from the Pan-Athenian procession

strongly identified with their community, where they were able to live free from foreign rule and according to their own laws. It was only those with full citizenship, however, who participated in political life in the form of direct democracy – in about 430 BC they accounted for approximately 13 per cent of the town's inhabitants who mostly belonged to the upper class and were exclusively male. To assure the independence of full citizens in the People's Law Courts and in the People's Assembly, a social policy stipulated daily payments (diets) for those with political office, for judges and members of the People's Assembly; cared for the lower classes through navy service, while shifting all production and services onto foreigners, those with fewer rights and slaves. Social pressure from a population explosion was relieved through the foundation of colonies. The production of sufficient food was assured through an active trading policy and the import and export of food, which at the same time kept the fleet busy at all times.

In the last 1600 years, both Acropolis and Agorá, witnesses to the cultural

blossoming and political strength of Athens, decayed with the fall of the town. Athena's gold-ivory statue remained in the Parthenon until the 5th century AD, when it was taken down in the process of Christianisation and probably taken to Constantinople where it was lost. In the 6th century, the Parthenon Temple was transformed into a Christian church. Under Turkish rule it served as a mosque, after a large part of the temple had been destroyed in 1687 when, during bombardment by the Venetians, the gun powder that had been stored there exploded. Between 1801 and 1803, with the agreement of the Turkish authorities, Lord Elgin acquired numerous metopes and sculptures from the Parthenon, the so-called Elgin Marbles. In 1816, the British government bought these artefacts and they are now on show in the collection of antiquities in the British Museum in London. The Greek governments, most recently in the 1980s through Melina Mercouri, have been demanding the return of the Elgin marbles as "symbol of the nation and part of a unique work of art". The British government, however, refused the release with the counter-argument that all important museums around the world, including the Greek museums, would stand empty if all exhibits that did not belong to their host nation were to be returned.

In order to appreciate today the former greatness of Athens during Classic times, this unique mixture of art, culture and politics, one would have to travel through half of Europe, for only fragments are on show locally and these would have to be complemented by the antiquity collections in the museums of the European capitals. Perhaps, within the framework of European unification, it will be possible to reassemble the many parts into one whole.

The awe-inspiring Propylaia at the entrance to the Acropolis

store. A bastion which was later built between the south wing and the platform bearing the temple of Athena Nike was removed in 1836, and the Frankish Tower, built in the 14 c. by the Florentine Duke of Athens, Nerio Acciaiuoli, was pulled down by Schliemann in 1875 at his own expense. Extensive restoration works began in 1909.

★Temple of Athena Nike

There was an ancient sanctuary dedicated to Athena as the bringer of victory (nike) on the spur of rock on the south side of the Propylaia – a rocky platform outside the Mycenaean walls.

The Temple of Athena Nike was built in 432–421, after the completion of the Parthenon and the Propylaia. It has four Ionic columns at the north and south ends. The form of the column bases and capitals was already old-fashioned at the time of the erection, leading Carpenter to suggest that after the end of the Periclean period the earlier design by Kallikrates was used.

In Turkish times (1686) the temple was thrown down to use the bastion as an artillery position, from which Ludwig Ross disengaged it in 1836. Re-erected at the time, and again after consolidation work between 1936 and 1940, it is the daintiest and most elegant building on the Acropolis. Its Ionic forms contrast with the Doric massiveness of the Propylaia and with the ancient masonry of the "Pelasgian" (i.e. Mycenaean) defensive walls which can be seen to the east.

The Acropolis Museum (see page 51) contains the balustrade from the temple platform, with relief figures of Athena and several representations of Nike (Victory).

Sanctuary of Athena Hygieia

Among the many sanctuaries which lay within the walls of the Acropolis and have left traces in the limestone of the crag was one sacred to Athena Hygieia. Beside the southern column of the east portico of the Propylaia is the semicircular base which once supported a bronze statue of the goddess. Opposite it is the square foundation of the altar. This sanctuary was built following the plague of 429 BC, in which Pericles numbered among its victims.

Exactly in the axis of the central gate of the Propylaia stood a bronze statue of Athena Promachos (the "Champion"), a famous work by Phidias erected in 454 BC which stood 9 m (30 ft) high. The statue was later taken to Constantinople, and was destroyed during the Crusaders' siege of the city in 1203. The goddess, whose lance was visible from the great distance, stood on a marble base, parts of which, with an unusually large "egg-and-dart" moulding, are still in situ.

Statue Athena Promachos

In the 6th c. BC Peisistratos brought the cult of Artemis to Athens from his home town of Brauron, and a sanctuary dedicated to this Artemis Brauronia was built in the south-west part of the Acropolis, within the Propylaia and the "Pelasgian" wall. The altar and the cult statue, by Praxiteles, stood in an open courtyard with colonnades on the south and east sides. The sanctuary was given its final form by Mnesikles when he built the Propylaia.

Brauronion

About 450 BC a hall was built immediately adjoining the Brauronion for the safe keeping of bronze votive offerings and weapons, and after 432 a colonnade was built along the north wall. Adjoining this was a flight of steps hewn from the rock leading up to the Parthenon, originally decked with numerous votive offerings, including a representation of the Trojan Horse.

Chalkotheke

This temple of Athena the Virgin (Athena Parthenos), built between 447 and 338 (the figures in the pediments being completed in 432), is the masterpiece of the architect Iktinos and the great sculptor Phidias, who was entrusted by Pericles with the general direction of the building operations on the Acropolis. The new Parthenon they built, however, was based on an earlier building on the same site.

★★Parthenon

On the basis of research by Hill, Dinsmoor and Carpenter the **history** of the building of the Parthenon can be summarised as follows:

490 BC (or soon after) The masonary foundation of the first Parthenon, standing up to 10.8 m (35 ft) high, were constructed, with 6 columns at the ends and 16 along the sides. At the time of the Persian attack in 480 it was still unfinished. The column drums were damaged in the burning of the Acropolis and were built into the Themistoclean north wall.

468 BC Kimon continued the construction of the temple, the "Pre-Parthenon", the architect being Kallikrates. On Kimon's death (450 BC) work was suspended.

447 BC Under Pericles, the new leader of Athens, the erection of the Parthenon proper began. Kallikrates was replaced by Iktinos, who used the building materials already available. The foundations were now adjusted to the new and wider ground plan. (On the south side of the Parthenon can be seen the older foundations, projecting further at the east end; the widening can also be observed in the northern part of the foundations at the west end.) The substructure (crepidoma) of the new temple consisted of three steps. There were now eight by seventeen columns, compared with the previous six and sixteen. The Doric columns are 10 m (33 ft) high. Note the entasis (swelling) of the columns and the curvature of the crepidoma, rising towards the middle (best seen on the top step, the stylobate). These optical refinements, like the slight inward inclination of the columns, with the corner columns leaning diagonally inward, were designed to relieve the rigidity and solidity of the building and create an effect of organic structure.

The roof was covered with marble tiles. The lions' heads at the eaves were solid and cannot therefore have been designed as water-spouts, in accordance with the usual practice; there were run-offs for rainwater at the four corners of the roof. The holes on the architrave of the east end mark the position of the pegs on which were hung the shields captured by Alexander the Great in the battle of the Granikos (334 BC) and dedicated by him to Athena.

The **interior** of the Parthenon – closed to visitors – is in two parts. At the west end is a rear chamber (opisthodomos), with traces of painting dating from the use of the Parthenon as a Christian church dedicated to the Virgin, leading into the temple proper, the roof of which was borne on four Ionic columns. This probably served as the state treasury.

At the east end is the pronaos, giving access to the chamber that contained the chryselephantine (gold and ivory) statue of Athena, a cult image known to us only from the descriptions and later copies. It was supported by a massive post, the hole for which can be seen in the floor of the cella.

The statue, completed in 438 BC, was one of Phidias' most renowned works, ranking with the figure of Athena Promachos on the Acropolis and that of Zeus in the Temple of Zeus at Olympia. It stood 12 m (39 ft) high, and the gold used in the dress and ornaments is said to have weighed about a ton; the gold was detachable, and could thus be removed to check the weight. The face and hands were of ivory. Like the Athena Promachos, the statue was carried off to Constantinople and was destroyed there in 1203.

Marks on the floor indicate that there was a two-storey colonnade on both sides and to the rear of the statue. Iktinos thus achieved a wholly new conception of the interior of a temple, which was no longer merely designed as a chamber to house the cult image. It has been supposed that the widening of the ground plan of the temple from six to eight columns was made necessary by this new conception, so that here, for the first time in a Greek temple, the interior chamber with the cult statue determined the whole plan of the structure.

No less celebrated than the cult statue was the sculpture on the **exterior** of the Parthenon – the two pediments, the Doric metopes and the Ionic frieze around the upper part of the cella wall. It is characteristic of the Parthenon that an Ionic feature of this kind was used in a Doric temple, reflecting a firm intention to link the two orders together: Periclean Athens was to be the point of crystallisation of Doric as well as Ionic Hellenism.

Some of the sculpture is still in situ, and there is some in the Acropolis Museum (see page 51). There is also some in the Louvre in Paris, but most of it is in the British Museum, having been transported to London by Lord Elgin in 1801.

The **pediments**, completed in 432 BC, depict the birth of Athena from the head of Zeus (east end) and the conflict between Athena and Poseidon for the land of Attica (west end). The east pediment now contains copies of Dionysos (on left) and the heads of the sun god's horses and the moon goddess (at both corners). The west pediment has the figure of king Kekrops with one of his daughters (original).

The 92 metopes of the **Doric frieze** depicted a fight with giants (east), a fight with centaurs (south the best preserved), a fight with Persians or with Amazons (west) and the Trojan War (north).

The **Ionic frieze** on the outer wall of the cella, 1 m (3 ft) high and 160 m (525 ft) long, is not devoted to mythical or historical subjects like the pediments and metopes but reflects the life of Athens in the Classical period. It depicts the Panathenaic festival, held every four years, when a great procession made its way from the Gymnasion at the Dipylon, by way of the Agora, to the Acropolis (see Agora, Panathenaic Way). The procession begins at the south-west corner, runs to the left along the west end, where the slabs bearing the reliefs are still in situ (with a recently erected protective roof), and then continues along the north side to the east end, where it meets the other half of the procession running along the south side. The object of the procession was to present a new peplos to the goddess Athena, who was depicted on the east end. The frieze is a masterly representation of the people of Athens playing their part in this great national religious occasion, with men, women, riders, sacrificial animals and officials, subtly organised in rhythmic groups, all moving towards their goal at a stately pace or in rapid advance.

Later history The Parthenon suffered considerable damage when in the 5th c., after serving as a temple for some 900 years, it was transformed into a Christian church dedicated to the Virgin. Among the changes then made was the construction of an apse, involving the destruction of the central group on the east pediment. The disfigurement of many of the metopes, on the basis of their "pagan" character, is no doubt also to be dated to the Christian period.

The Parthenon remained in use as a church for some 950 years before becoming a Turkish mosque in 1456. The only changes made by the Turks were the removal of the Christian additions and the construction of a minaret at the south-west corner – 231 years later a Venetian grenade blew up the powder magazine which the Turks had installed in the Parthenon, and the building which had stood for more than 2100 years was destroyed. A small mosque was later built in the ruins. In the 19th c. this was removed, as were all the other Turkish and Crusader structures on the Acropolis, leaving the Parthenon a ruin but a purely Greek one.

The Erechtheion, built between 421 and 395 BC and thus the youngest feature of the Acropolis in its classical form, incorporates a number of very ancient sanctuaries, and its complicated ground plan reflects the need to take account of these earlier structures. ★★Erechtheion

The eastern part was occupied by the temple of Athena Polias, patron of the city, with the ancient and much venerated wooden cult figure (xoanon) which had previously stood in the Old Temple of Athena, no doubt perpetuating cult traditions going back to the palace that occupied the site in Mycenaean times.

In the western part of the Erechtheion were the tombs of king Erechtheus, who gave his name to the whole structure, and Kekrops, the mythical founder of the Athenian royal line. The tomb of Kekrops lay under the **Porch of the Caryatids** which projects on the south side of the Erechtheion, its entablature borne by six figures of maidens in place of columns.

On the north side is another cult feature. An opening in the floor affords a view of the rock in which the ancient Athenians saw the trident wielded by Poseidon when contending with Athena for possession of Attica.

The east and north porticos each had six Ionic columns, though the east portico now lacks one of its columns, which Lord Elgin carried off to London together with one of the caryatids and the rest of the "Elgin marbles".

The doorway leading from the north portico into the interior of the temple is a masterpiece of rich and delicate ornament. On the outer side of the cella wall, above elegant palmette ornament, is a frieze of grey Eleusinian marble on which were set white marble figures (originals in the Acropolis Museum).

The building was altered during the Roman period, in particular the west side, which then received its two-storey form. It suffered further alterations in the 7th c., when it became a Christian church. In 1463 the Turkish commandant of the fortress used it for the accommodation of his harem. The result of these changes was that the interior lost its original division into the temple of Athena Polias

The Parthenon, an architectural masterpiece of the 5th c. BC, is a symbol of the power and wealth of ancient Athens

to the east and the western part with the tomb of Erechtheus. Most of the exterior, with its delicate Ionic ornament, has survived.

From the north portico a side doorway leads into the adjoining cult precinct of the Pandroseion (see page 51), which in turn is adjoined on the south by the foundation walls of the Old Temple of Athena, lying under the Porch of the Caryatids.

To the east of the Erechtheion stood the altar belonging to this earlier temple.

The Erechtheion is at present being taken down in order to consolidate and re-erect the structure in accordance with the best conservational practice. The caryatids are temporarily housed in the Acropolis Museum (see page 51).

Porch of the Caryatids

Old Temple of Athena

The Old Temple of Athena, also known as the Hekatompedon because its cella measured 32.8 by 16.4 m (100 by 50 ft), was built in the early 6th c. BC within the precincts of the Mycenaean royal palace of the 14th c. BC (now represented only by two column bases from its megaron, protected by gratings). The cella had no surrounding colonnade. The great pediment of poros limestone in the Acropolis Museum (Rooms II and III, see entry) probably came from this temple; it depicts in the centre bulls being attacked by lions, on the left Herakles and Triton, on the right a monster with three bodies (Nereus?). Around 525 BC Peisistratos built a temple with a colonnade of 6 by 12 columns, either a reconstruction of the Hekatompedon or an entirely new structure. In the pediment figures, depicting Athena in a fight with giants, marble was used for the first time on the Acropolis (see Acropolis Museum, Room V). This "Old Temple" superseded the Hekatompedon as the sanctuary of Athena Polias and took over the old wooden cult image of the goddess.

The temple was destroyed by the Persians in 480 BC together with all the other buildings of the Archaic period. In 406 BC the remains were razed to the ground after the transfer of the cult image to the new temple of Athena in the eastern part of the Erechtheion.

The foundations of the temple were brought to light in the 19th c.; they can be seen immediately south of the Erechtheion.

House of Arrhephoroi

This house, a rectangular structure built against the north wall of the Acropolis with a porch and a courtyard to the left, was occupied by four girls between the ages of seven and eleven from the noblest families in Athens who assisted the priestess of Athena in serving the goddess. One of their duties was to make the new peplos worn by Athena at each four-yearly celebration of the Panathenaic festival (see Agora, Panathenaic Way).

From the courtyard a flight of steps led down through a gate in the outer wall of the Acropolis and a rock-cut passage to the sanctuary of Eros and the Cave of Aglauros, from which the Arrhephoroi had to fetch some secret cult objects (hence their name, "bearers of holy things").

A structure further to the west along the north wall is believed to have been the house of the priestess of Apollo.

In the obtuse angle between the Erechtheion and the Old Temple of Athena is the Pandroseion, a shrine named after Pandrosos, daughter of the first king of Athens, Kekrops, and sister of Herse and Aglauros, to whom one of the sacred caves on the north side of the Acropolis was dedicated (see Cave of Aglauros). The sanctuary was a rectangular courtyard enclosed by walls in which stood an altar of Zeus Herkeios (protector of the hearth) and no doubt also a small temple of Pandrosos. It was probably here too that the sacred snakes of the Acropolis were kept. At the south-east corner was an access to the tomb of Kekrops. Here too grew the sacred olive-tree presented to the city by Athena after her victory over Poseidon in the contest for the land of Attica. Herodotus (VIII, 55) tells us that on the day after the destruction of the Acropolis by the Persians in 480 BC a fresh shoot a cubit long had sprung from the trunk of the burned tree, giving an assurance of the continued survival of Athens. The memory of this olive-tree is perpetuated by a new tree planted here in modern times.

Pandroseion

In 27 BC the Romans built, outside the east end of the Parthenon and on its central axis, a circular temple on a square tufa substructure. The roof was borne by nine Ionic columns, with capitals painstakingly modelled on those of the Erechtheion. The temple contained statues of Rome and Augustus, to whom it was dedicated.

Temple of Rome and Augustus

North-east of the Parthenon and north of the temple of Rome and Augustus is the highest point on the Acropolis, which was occupied by the sanctuary of Zeus Polieus, an open cult precinct (temenos) containing an altar and a stable for the sacrificial animals (Boukoleion). The only remains of the sanctuary are cuttings in the rock.

Sanctuary of Zeus Polieus

This terrace at the north-east corner of the Acropolis was laid out for the royal family in the 19th c., and affords a good view of the city looking towards Sýntagma Square and the Parliament (see entries).

★Belvedere

The Acropolis Museum, containing one of the most valuable collections of Greek art in existence, was built in 1949–53 at the south-east corner of the Acropolis, lying so low that it does not obtrude. The rooms to the left contain material of the Archaic period (6th c. BC) that formed part of the "Persian rubble" and was recovered during excavations by Panayiotis Kavvadias in 1885–6: pediments from temples and treasuries, votive statues and (in the rooms to the right) marble figures from the pediment of the Old Temple of Athena (Rooms I–V). In the other rooms to the right (VI–XI) is sculpture of the Classical period (5th c.).

★★Acropolis Museum

The **Vestibule** is dominated by a large owl, the emblem of Athena (early 5th c. BC). Here, too, are a marble statue of Athena, "Athena Propylaia" (end of 5th c.); a marble base with a relief of soldiers dancing (4th c. BC) and a marble funerary lekythos (end of 4th c.). The caryatids from the Erechtheion are temporarily housed in a room to the right.

Room I (Early 6th c. BC): to the left is a pediment group in painted poros limestone depicting Herakles fighting the Lernaean hydra (c. 600 BC).

Opposite the entrance is a lioness rending a young bull, from a large poros pediment (c. 490 BC); to the right is a Gorgon (early 6th c. BC).

Room II Introduction of Herakles to Olympus (c. 580 BC).

The right-hand half of the "Red Pediment", depicting Herakles and Triton (c. 560 BC).

The "Olive-tree Pediment", probably portraying the myth of Troilos, with a representation of a temple and a girl carrying water (c. 570 BC).

Two sections of a poros pediment, probably from the old Temple of Athena: to the left Harakles and Triton, to the right a three-bodied monster, now believed to be Nereus (580–570 BC). The central section of the pediment was probably the group of two lions rending a bull displayed in Room II.

Here, too, are the famous Moschoporos ("Calf-Bearer") of Hymettian marble, a votive offering by Rhombos (c. 570 BC), and the earliest of the korai, the figures of girls which were set up in large numbers on the Acropolis as votive offerings to Athena; in one hand this Attic work holds a pomegranate, in the other a garland (early 6th c. BC).

Room III Central section of a pediment group (cf. Room II) and the torsos of two other korai, probably from Naxos or Samos (580–550 BC).

Room IV This room contains a large number of master works. First come four or perhaps five works attributed to the same sculptor, Phaidimos. The earliest is the so-called Rampin Horseman, the head of which is a cast (original in the Louvre). Together with a second horseman preserved in fragments this formed the earliest known equestrian group in Greece. It is believed to represent either Hippias and Hipparchos, the sons of Peisistratos, or the Dioscuri (c. 550 BC).

A famous mature work by the same sculptor is the "Peplos Kore" (c. 530 BC) named after the Doric garment which she wears. A lion-head spout from the Old Temple of Athena (c. 525 BC) and a hound from the Brauronion (c. 520 BC) are also attributed to Phaidimos.

A figure of a horseman in Persian or Scythian costume probably represents Miltiades (c. 520 BC).

In the rear part of Room IV are a group of korai, wearing the peplos or later the more elegant chiton, usually covered with the himation (cloak). As a rule one hand gathers in the maiden's garment while the other holds a votive offering. These figures, mostly life-size, stood in the open air, and many of them still preserve the fixing of the meniskos, an iron shield designed to protect them from bird droppings. The figures were originally painted, and some traces of colouring can still be seen, particularly on the garments.

First come a kore with a serious expression, wearing Ionic costume (520–510 BC), a graceful kore from Chios in an elegantly draped painted chiton (c. 510 BC) and a very fine head (c. 510 BC).

Then, in a wide semicircle, are (from left to right) a large kore from Chios (c. 520 BC), a vigorous figure, probably from the Peloponnese (c. 490 BC), the enigmatic "Sphinx-Eyed Kore" (c. 500 BC) and a kore clad only in a chiton (c. 510 BC).

A large and badly weathered seated figure of Athena (in the centre of the group) by Endoios (c. 530 BC) is followed by the clothed figure of a youth (end of 6th c. BC), a severe kore, the only one not girding her garment (c. 500 BC), an almost unworn kore from the Ionian Islands (c. 520 BC) and a large kore, also almost undamaged (c. 520 BC).

Room V The most notable item is the Kore of Antenor, 2 m (6 ft) high, standing on a base bearing the name of the donor, Nearchos, and the sculptor, Antenor, which probably does not belong to it (c. 525 BC).

The room is dominated by statues from the pediment of the Peisistratid Old Temple depicting Athena fighting giants (c. 525 BC).

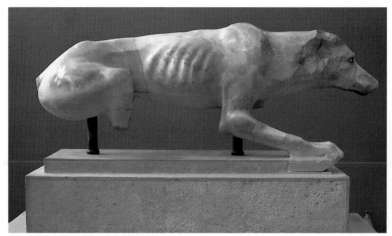

Figure of a hound from the Brauronian

In the alcove to the left is a collection of pottery ranging in date from the Geometric to the late Classical period.

Room VI The earliest works belonging to this first stage of classical art date from before the Persian conquest (480 BC). This room contains work of this phase together with examples of the "Severe" style.

Among outstanding items are the "Sulky Kore" (*c*. 490 BC), dedicated by Euthydikos; the "Kore of the Propylaia", set up shortly before the Persian attack (*c*. 480 BC); a statue of Athena (480–470 BC); a relief figure of a potter (*c*. 500 BC); the head of a youth, from the workshop of Phidias (450–440 BC); and the forequarters of a horse, a noble work of 490–480 BC. Famous works of the early Classical period are the "Fair-Haired Youth", a figure of unusual melancholy beauty (shortly before 480 BC); a relief of "Mourning Athena" (460–450 BC); and the oldest of the group, the figure of a boy ascribed to Kritios or his workshop (485 BC). The torso and head of this "Critian Boy" were found in 1865 and 1888. It is the earliest known figure in which the archaic posture with each leg bearing an equal weight gives place to the classical pose in which one leg bears the weight and the other hangs free. In this respect Kritios was a forerunner of the art of the Classical period.

The following rooms are devoted to the buildings of the Classical period on the Acropolis.

Room VII Plaster reproductions of the Parthenon pediments, a metope from the south side (centaurs and Lapiths), a torso of Poseidon from the west pediment and two horses' heads from Poseidons team.

Room VIII Large sections of the Parthenon frieze, 160 m (525 ft) long, depicting the great Panathenaic procession (see Agora and giving a vivid impression of life in Athens in the age of Pericles.

From the north frieze: horsemen, apobatai (who jump off and on moving chariots), marshals, musicians, youths, carrying hydrias and sacrificial animals. The last slab is undoubtedly the work of Phidias himself.

From the south frieze: horsemen.

From the east frieze: Poseidon, Apollo and Artemis, probably carved by Alkamenes, a pupil of Phidias.

On the projecting wall which divides the room into two are parts of the Erechtheion frieze, carved some decades after the Parthenon frieze (between 409 and 405 BC). The reconstruction shows the techniques used, the figures in light-coloured Pentelic marble being attached to the background of darker marble with metal pegs. The significance of the figures is unclear.

Finally there are a series of slabs from the parapet round the temple of Athena Nike (c. 410 BC). The reliefs, which originally decorated the outer side of the parapet, depict a seated Athena with a number of goddesses of victory, including the famous Nike losing her sandal.

Relief of Athena

Room IX A large mask of a deity, a bas-relief of an Attic trireme and – the most notable item – an idealised portrait of the young Alexander, probably carved by Leochares or Euphranor after Alexander's visit to Athens in 335 BC. Also very beautiful is the marble group "Procne and Itys" by Alkamenes.

Caves

On the northern slopes of the Acropolis are a number of caves that in ancient times were dedicated to the cult of the gods. Near the west end, close together, are three such caves, two of them sacred to Apollo, the third to Pan. They were originally accessible from the Acropolis by a flight of steps.

The most easterly of the three, lying below the House of the Arrhephoroi, is the **Cave of Aglauros**, in which sacred festivals were celebrated with music and dancing. Here, too, the ephebes swore their oath.

The cave is named after Aglauros, one of the three daughters of Kekrops. She and her sister Herse opened a casket which had been entrusted to them by Athena, although they had been forbidden to tamper with it: whereupon they lost their reason and sprang to their deaths from the summit of the Acropolis. The third of the sisters, Pandrosos, escaped this fate and has a sanctuary dedicated to her on the Acropolis (see Pandroseion, above).

The most westerly, the **Cave of Apollo Hypoakraios**, was sacred to Apollo Hypoakraios. The site of the altar was found outside the entrance, and in the walls of the cave are small niches with votive inscriptions.

A little way east is another cave which was also dedicated to Apollo. Here he seduced Kreousa, who later abandoned her son Ion in the cave.

In the eastern part of this cave a chapel dedicated to St Athanasius was installed in Christian times.

The largest cave, the **Cave of Pan**, was sacred to the old shepherd god Pan, who was particularly honoured in Athens after the Persian wars, since the Athenian victory of Marathon (490 BC) was attributed to his aid.

Sanctuary of Eros and Aphrodite

Numerous votive tablets found in caves on the northern face of the Acropolis indicate that there was a sanctuary of Eros and Aphrodite here. In this area (below the Erechtheion to the north-east, outside the walls) stood the "temple of Aphrodite in the gardens" mentioned by Pausanias – to be distinguished from a temple of the same name, but probably of later date, on the Ilissos. This temple could be reached from the Acropolis by a flight of steps still visible north-east of the Erechtheion.

Going up towards the Acropolis from Dionysíou Areopagitou Street (where the tourist buses stop), not on the broad paved way but on the footpath beside the Odeion of Herodes Atticus, we see on the left a tri-angular marble pillar with an inscription commemorating the French general Baron Nicolas Favier (1782–1855) and Major Frank Robert, who defended the Acropolis against the Turks in 1826.

Monument to Philhellenes

★★Aegina

Area of the island: 83 sq. km (32 sq. mi.)
Altitude: 0–532 m (0–1746 ft)
Population: 11,000
Chief town: Aíyina

Hydrofoils ply several times a day between Piraeus and the ports of Aegina, Suvála and Ayía Marína, as well as between Méthana and Aegina. There are also local boat trips to Ankístri and day-cruises from Piraeus and Páleo Fáliro to the islands of Aegina, Poros and Hýdra.

Ferries

Aegina (Aíyina, Saronic Island), known as Aigina in ancient times, 19 km (12 mi.) south-west of Piraeus in the Saronic Gulf, is a fertile, hilly island of tertiary marlaceous limestone and slate, dotted with hills of volcanic origin. Few sheltered bays are to be found along the mainly steep coastline. The inhabitants gain their living from agriculture, mainly the cultivation and export of pistachio nuts. Fishing, diving for sponges, and pottery are also important industries; the locally made vessels for cooling water, known as kannatia, are twin-handled, wide-necked jugs which keep their contents cool by evaporation through the porous top. The mild climate and low rainfall have made the island a favourite summer retreat for upmarket Athenians for many years, and more recently it has also attracted numbers of tourists.

History According to legend Aeakos, the son of Aegina and father of Peleus and Telamon who was elected a judge of the underworld together with Minos and Rhadamanthys because of his wise and just rule, was the progenitor of the Aeginians.
   The oldest signs of Pelasgic settlement date back to the third millen-nium BC. By the year 2000 BC the island was already an important trading centre for pottery and ointments, as shown by finds from the Helladic, Cycladic and Minoan regions. History first mentions Aegina as a colony of Epidauros and under the rule of the Phaidon of Argos in the 7th c. BC. When it became independent in the 6th. c. BC it flourished in competition with Corinth. Trading posts were established in central Italy, on the Black Sea and in Egypt, and the island's shipowners became some of the richest in Greece. Aeginian coins embossed with a turtle were some of the oldest known and were widely used as early as 656 BC Aeginian weights and measures were used until Roman times.
   At the beginning of the Persian Wars this sea-faring state was at its height. After the Battle of Salamis (480 BC), to which the island sent thirty ships, a ship from Aegina received a prize for bravery. However, it is known that trading interests in fact led the Aeginians to offer the enemy land and sea rights in return for their surrender, and they were called to account for their actions by Sparta at the request of Athens. This was followed by further disputes with Athens, to whom the island

presented an obstacle in its quest for greater power at sea. Ensuing victories by the Athenian forces at Kekryphaleia (Ankristi) and off Aegina itself proved decisive: in spite of having to fight simultaneous campaigns in Megara and Egypt, in 456 BC the Athenians forced the town to surrender after a nine-month siege, and it was made to tear down its walls, hand over its fleet of warships and pay tribute to Athens.

At the start of the Peloponnese War in 431 BC the people of Aegina were driven from their island and the land divided up among the citizens of Attica. Although the people were able to return after the fall of Athens in 404 BC the island's heyday was over. Fresh campaigns by a re-strengthened Attica brought Aegina once again under its sway, and henceforth the island was to share in its destinies.

Aíyina, the island's chief town, was the capital of Greece from January 12th to October 3rd 1828.

Aíyina Town

The island's capital, with a population of 5000, lies on a gentle slope around a wide bay on the north-western coast, approximately on the site of a more extensive ancient town. From the harbour, which is protected by breakwaters, there is a beautiful view of the smaller islands of Metópi and Ankístri to the south-west, Moni to the south, and of the Epidauros mountain range.

The Archaeological Museum contains grave-finds dating from the 3rd millennium BC up to Roman times, especially from the Temples of Aphaia and Aphrodite.

Kolóna

On Kolóna Hill north of the present town stands a Doric column thought to be from the Temple of Aphrodite (460 BC) near the harbour, which was originally dedicated to Apollo. Below the temple have been found traces of pre-Mycenaean and Mycenaean settlements (3rd c. BC), and to the west two smaller temples, probably those of Artemis and Dionysos. The "Aeginian Sphinx", dating from c. 460 BC, which was found here in 1904, can now be seen in the Archaeological Museum.

Ancient harbour

Below the temple to the south was once the ancient harbour, now silted, the quay of which is still visible below the water on calm days. The modern harbour, on the site of the old military port, is protected by the old breakwaters which have been kept in a good state of repair. On the longer breakwater to the north stands a chapel dedicated to St Nicholas, dating from the early 19th c.

Grave of Phokos

Some 1½ km (1 mi.) north of the town stands a 6th c. tumulus similar to that of Sorós in Marathon, believed to be the grave of Phokos, half-brother of Peleus and Telamon.

★★Temple of Aphaia

Open Mon.–Fri.
8am–5pm, Sat.,
Sun., pub. hols.
8.30am–3pm

Admission fee

The Temple of Aphaia stands 13 km (8 mi.) east of the town of Aíyina. The road leading to it takes us through partly wooded, partly built-up hilly terrain. First we pass the Church of Agii Theodori, built from remains of an ancient temple; note the frescoes dating from 1289. After 8 km (5 mi.) we come to the old medieval island capital of Palaeochóra (abandoned in 1800), with some 20 chapels from the 13th–18th c. Above lie the ruins of the medieval kastro, and further still the scattered houses of Mesagró. Finally a steep path brings us to the temple.

This temple, dating from the 5th c BC, is dedicated to Aphaia, a god-

The Temple of Aphaia on the island of Aegina

dess regarded as the protectress of the Women of Artemis; note the dedicatory inscriptions in terracotta. The building rests on the foundations of a 6th c. BC sanctuary and is on the site of a pre-Greek cult site, being laid out in peripteral style with a colonnade of 6 by 12 columns. The pronaos and opisthodom were enclosed by ante-walls with two columns in between. Inside the cella the roof is supported by two rows of columns. The opisthodom contains a stone altar-table. In the main, 23 columns of yellow limestone have been preserved, with parts of the original stucco facing, particularly on the east front and the adjoining sides, some being formed from a single block of stone. The

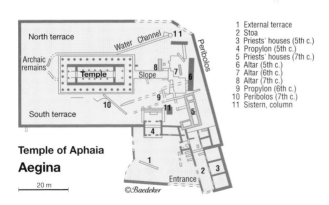

1 External terrace
2 Stoa
3 Priests' houses (5th c.)
4 Propylon (5th c.)
5 Priests' houses (7th c.)
6 Altar (5th c.)
7 Altar (6th c.)
8 Altar (7th c.)
9 Propylon (6th c.)
10 Peribolos (7th c.)
11 Sistern, column

Temple of Aphaia

Aegina

20 m

©Baedeker

roof and pediment figures were of marble. Unique are the uneven floor and the division of the opisthodom. In the floor are holes protected by grilles.

The marble pediment sculptures now housed in the Glyptothek in Munich were purchased by Crown Prince Ludwig of Bavaria in 1828. Other such figures can be seen in the museums in Athens and Aegina.

The sacrificial altar was as wide as the east front of the temple, and was connected to it by a ramp. To the south of the east front stands the little propylaeon, with octagonal pillars. The whole of the sacred area was levelled off with earth and supported in part by natural rock, in part by ashlar walls.

Around the temple can be seen remains of Late Neolithic dwellings from the 4th–3rd c. BC.

From the temple there is a fine **view** over much of the Saronic Gulf, extending from the Athens coast to Cape Soúnion.

Ayía Marína

3 km (2 mi.) south of the Temple of Aphaia, in a wide bay on the north-east coast of Aegina, lies the busy, modern seaside resort of Ayía Marína.

Oros

The Oros ("Mountain", 532 m (1750 ft)), also known as Profitis Ilías (Prophet Elijah) because of a chapel on the top dedicated to the prophet, is the island's highest point. A difficult footpath leads up to it from the little town of Marathon, 6 km (4 mi.) south of Aegina. In Mycenaean times (13th c. BC) there was a large town on the terraces around the mountain peak, protected by walls of large irregular blocks. To the north, below the peak near the chapel dedicated to Taxiarchis, once stood the old temple in which Zeus Panhellenios was worshipped in the 5th. c. BC.

There is a fine **view** from here over almost the whole island and the Saronic Gulf, taking in Salamis, the Methurides (Trupika and Rhevitusa), Diaporia, Ankístri, the Methana peninsula, the island of Poros and extending as far as Hýdra.

Ankístri

About 5 km (3 mi.) south-west of Aegina lies the wooded island of Ankístri, covering an area of 12 sq. km (4½ sq. mi.), and ranging from 0–216 m (0–710 ft) above sea level. Its 700 or so inhabitants are descendants of 16th c. Albanian immigrants.

Agora   K 7

Location
Between Leofóros
Apostólou Pávlou
and Adrianoú

Electric Railway
Theseion and
Monastiráki
stations

Open Tue.–Sun.
8.30am–2.45pm

Admission fee

In the north of the Acropolis (see entry) there are three large open areas – the Agora, the principal market-place of ancient Athens, the Roman Agora (see entry) and Hadrian's Library (see entry).

A good general impression of the Agora can be obtained from four viewpoints: the north wall of the Acropolis, the Areopagos, the road that runs east from the Areopagos along the north side of the Acropolis, and the road along the north side of the Areopagos. The detailed layout of the Agora can best be appreciated by entering the site at the north gate, off Adrianoú Street (near the church of St Philip), and consulting the plan displayed just inside the entrance.

History From the Mycenaean period until the end of the 7th c. BC this was a cemetery area. It began to be used as an agora during the early 6th c., in the time of Solon, and the oldest buildings were erected at the west end of the site, under the Agora Hill. Thereafter it remained for many centuries the centre of the city's public life, each century erecting new buildings, frequently at the expense of earlier ones. In AD 267 numerous buildings were destroyed and c. AD 400 a

View from the Acropolis of the Agora with the Temple of Hephaistos

new Gymnasion was built, which served as Athen's University until 529.

The Agora was excavated by American archaeologists in 1931–41 and 1946–60 after the demolition of a whole district of the city comprising some 400 buildings which had grown up since the 11th c., and the remains have been incorporated in an attractive park. Since 1970 further excavations have been carried out north of the Piraeus railway, which previously formed the boundary of the excavation site, and to the east of the Agora, where, under a modern road, excavation has brought to light the ancient road linking the Agora with the Roman market, together with the buildings flanking the road. A few years ago US archaeologists succeeded in unearthing parts of the "Stoá Poikile" or "Painted Hall".

According to Pausanias (VIII, 2, 1) the Panathenaic festival in honour of Athena was instituted by Theseus. From the time of Peisistratos (6th c. BC) it was celebrated every four years on the 28th day of the month of Hekatombaion (July–August), Athena's birthday. Starting from the Pompeion in the Kerameikos (see entry), the great Panathenaic procession made its way through the Agora and up to the Acropolis (see entry).

Panathenaic Way

Considerable stretches of the old processional way, with paving of the 2nd c. BC, are still preserved within the area of the Agora, entering the excavation site at the Altar of the Twelve Gods (see page 65) and running south-east from there.

The most prominent feature on the east side of the Agora is the Stoa of Attalos, built by king Attalos II of Pergamon (160–139 BC), brother and successor to Eumenes II, who built the Stoa of Eumenes on the south side of the Acropolis. The stoa was (and is, since the faithful reconstruction of the original building in 1953–56) two-storeyed, with Doric columns fronting the lower floor and Ionic columns on the upper floor.

★Stoa of Attalos

Agora

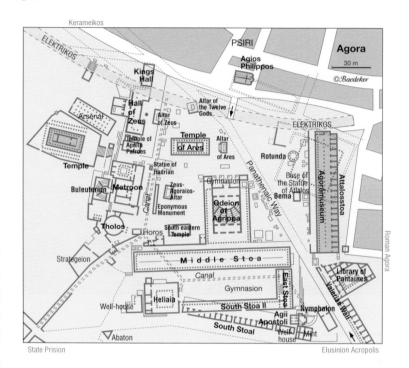

The stoa proper, which is backed by a series of rectangular rooms (originally 21), is divided by Ionic columns into two aisles. The reconstruction has restored the impressive spatial effect of the long pillared hall. In ancient times the stoa was occupied by offices and shops; it now houses the Agora Museum.

In front of the stoa, near the north end, are remains of a small hall and a circular fountain-house. Half-way along are an orator's rostrum (bema) and the base which bore a statue of Attalos II.

Agora Museum

The Agora Museum is housed in the reconstruction (1953–6) of the Stoa of Attalos, originally built in the 2nd c. BC The wealth of material recovered during the Agora excavations is displayed in the two-aisled stoa and the rooms to the rear.

The display of sculpture begins at the south end with the colossal statue of Apollo Patroos (4th c. BC), ascribed by Pausanias to the sculptor Euphranor. Then follow a painted Ionic capital (5th c. BC); two statues (opposite the second column) representing the Iliad and the Odyssey (early 2nd c. AD); a priestess (opposite the fourth column: 4th c. BC), flanked by two herms, the one on the right with a hand resting on it which, like Praxiteles' Hermes at Olympia, bears a child (Roman); a marble stele inscribed with a law against tyranny and a relief depicting Democracy crowning the people of Athens (by the fifth column: 336 BC);

60

sculpture from the Temple of Hephaistos (opposite the eleventh column); and acroteria from the Stoa of Zeus (at north end).

Rear hall The long main hall to the rear displays in chronological order a large collection of material, most of it notable not so much for its artistic quality as for the evidence it gives on life in ancient Athens.

The collection begins with material of the Neolithic period (3rd millennium BC).

The Mycenaean period (1500–1100 BC) is represented by vases and grave goods, including two ivory caskets carved with griffins and nautiluses.

Material of the early Iron Age (11th–8th c. BC) includes two 9th c. tombs with their grave goods and Proto-Geometric and Geometric vases. Then come vases in Orientalising style, a mould for casting a bronze statue dating from the Archaic period (6th c. BC) and a beautiful 6th c. terracotta figure of a kneeling boy.

Here, too, are large numbers of items illustrating the everyday life of the Classical period (5th c. BC) – inscriptions, a machine for the selection of public officials by lot, sherds used in the process of ostracism (among the names inscribed being that of Themistokles), etc.

On either side of the exit are finds from a well, ranging in date from the 1st to the 10th c. AD, and material of the Byzantine and Turkish periods.

The remains of this library, built by Flavius Pantaenus in AD 100 and destroyed by the Herulians in 267, lie immediately south of the Stoa of Attalos, separated from it by the road leading to the Roman Agora (see entry).

Library of Pantainos

The Valerian Wall was a late Roman defensive wall built after the Herulian invasion of AD 267, using the remains of destroyed buildings. Fragments can be seen to the south of the Library of Pantainos (see above) and to the east of the Ayii Apóstoli church (see entry).

Valerian Wall

In the 2nd c. AD a semicircular fountain-house, the Nymphaion, was built at the south-east corner of the Agora, in an area occupied by a number of older buildings: immediately south-west a fountain-house (the Enneakrounos?) of the 6th c. BC, adjoining this a 5th c. structure which was probably a mint (argyrokopeion), and to the east a temple dating from the early Roman period. Columns and probably also the cult image from the Doric temple of Demeter and Kore in Thorikos (5th c. BC) were used in the construction of this temple; remains of the structure were built into the late Roman "Valerian Wall" (see above).

Nymphaion

Above the Nymphaion stands the church of Ayii Apóstoli. The Church of the Holy Apostles was the only building left standing when the whole of this quarter of the city was pulled down to permit the excavation of the Agora (see entry). Originally built in the 10th c. over a circular nymphaion (sacred spring) and subsequently much altered, it has been reconstructed in its original form. The exterior is notable for its good ashlar masonry and the ornamental use of Kufic inscriptions.

Ayii Apóstoli

The dome is borne on four columns, and the apse and transepts have semicircular conches. There are well-preserved frescoes of Christ Pantocrator (Ruler of All: in the dome), John the Baptist, cherubim and archangels. Parts of the original 11th c. iconostasis have been preserved. The paintings in the narthex (c. 1700) are from St Spyridon's Church.

The American excavations have revealed a number of stoas (porticos serving various public purposes) in the southern part of the Agora.

Stoas

South Stoa I, lying between the earlier Heliaia and fountainhouse, was built between 425 and 400 BC. Situated on the road which bounded the

Agora on the south, it was a two-aisled portico with a series of small rooms to the rear.

In the 2nd c. BC South Stoa II was built, partly overlapping the site of the first one. This was a single-aisled portico with 30 Doric columns along the open north side.

The **Middle Stoa** was built between 175 and 150 BC. Open on all sides, with Doric columns around the perimeter supporting the roof, this was divided into two aisles by Ionic columns.

The **East Stoa**, open on the east side, was built about 150 BC (after the Middle Stoa but before South Stoa II). Like the other stoas, it was destroyed in 86 BC by the Romans under Sulla and thereafter served as a quarry for builders in quest of marble.

Heliaia

The Heliaia, a court established by Solon in the 6th c. BC, had its meeting-place on the south side of the Agora. It was named after the sun god Helios because it held its sessions before sunrise. There are remains of a large rectangular structure, on the north side of which can be seen a klepsydra (water-clock) and, on the west side, a fountain-house with two wings meeting at right angles.

Odeion of Agrippa

A well-preserved Corinthian capital of imposing dimensions marks the position of the Odeion of Agrippa, in the centre of the Agora. Built about 20 BC by the Roman general Agrippa, Augustus' son-in-law, it was a rectangular building with a stage and 18 tiers of seating that could accommodate an audience of 1000 (some remains preserved). The entrance was on the south side.

In the 2nd c. AD a new entrance was constructed on the north side, with three tritons and three giants supporting the roof of the portico; three of these figures are still erect.

Gymnasion

After the destruction of the original building by the Herulians in AD 267 the site was used in about 400 for the erection of a Gymnasion to house the University of Athens, which was closed down by the Emperor Justinian in 529; the foundations of this building can still be seen. Various university buildings were built further south.

Great Drain

The Great Drain was constructed in the early 5th c. BC to channel the rainwater which flowed down from the Acropolis and Areopagos (see entries) into the Eridanos. From the south-west end of the Agora it runs north-east and then bears north passing in front of the buildings on the west side of Agora.

Horos

At the point where the drain turns north and is joined by a subsidiary channel coming from the south-east stands the Horos, or boundary stone of the Agora, which was set up around 500 BC to show where the sacred area begins. Only free citizens with no criminal record could enter the Agora, and they had to undergo a ritual cleansing before doing so.

Tholos

The most southerly building on the west side of the Agora is the Tholos, a circular structure 18.3 m (60 ft) in diameter. Built around 465 BC on the site of an earlier rectangular building, this originally housed the sacred hearth and was the meeting-place of the 50 prytaneis (senators – representatives elected by the various tribes in the city state) of Athens, a third of whom were required to be in attendance at all times, even during the night; they were accordingly provided with meals and sleeping accommodation in the Tholos.

The roof of the Tholos was supported on six columns. In the 3rd c. BC a portico was added on the east side. Rebuilt after its destruction by Sulla in 86 BC, the building remained in use until about AD 450. Only the floor of the Tholos now remains, with an altar in the middle.

The Temple of Hephaistos is one of the best-preserved Greek temples

From the Agora an attractive footpath runs past the Tholos (see above) up the Agora Hill (Kolonos Agoraios), on which stands the Temple of Hephaistos. The erroneous name of Theseion still stubbornly persists (and is perpetuated by the name of the nearby station on the Piraeus railway); but the actual location of the real Theseion, in which the remains of the Attic hero Theseus were deposited after being brought back by Kimon from the island of Skyros in 475 BC, remains unknown.

★★Temple of Hephaistos

The Hephaisteion, lying near the smiths' and craftmen's quarter of Athens, was dedicated to the divinities of the smiths and the arts, Hephaistos and Athena. It is one of the best preserved of surviving Greek temples, thanks to the conversion into a Christian church which saved it from destruction.

This Doric temple, with the classical plan of six by thirteen columns, was built about the same time as the Parthenon (see Acropolis) but is considerably smaller. It has, however, certain features (e.g. Ionic friezes instead of Doric triglyphs on the façades of the pronaos and opisthodomos) which appear to be modelled on the Parthenon. The explanation is that building began, probably under the direction of Kallikrates, before 449 BC but was suspended to allow concentration of effort on Pericles' great building programme on the Acropolis and resumed only during the Peace of Nikias (421–415 BC), after Pericles' death.

This late date explains the more recent aspect of the east end, with the entrance to the temple. Here the portico, the coffered ceiling of which is completely preserved, is three bays deep (compared with one and a half at the west end) and is tied in to the axis of the third column; the pronaos frieze is carried across to the north and south peristyles; and the metopes have carved decoration, while elsewhere they are plain. All these features are innovations which give greater emphasis to the east end, departing from the earlier principle of a balance between the two ends.

Agora

The damaged **pronaos frieze** depicts battle scenes, the west frieze fighting between Lapiths and centaurs (in the middle the invulnerable Lapith Kaineus being driven into the ground by centaurs).

In spite of its small size, the **cella** had columns round three sides framing the cult images of Hephaistos and Athena (by Alkamenes) which were set up in the temple about 420 BC, this also in imitation of the Parthenon. The cella walls were roughened and covered with paintings.

When in the 5th c. the temple was converted into a Christian **church**, dedicated to St George, it became necessary to construct a chancel at the east end in place of the previous entrance. A new entrance (still preserved) was therefore broken through the west wall of the cella, and the old east entrance wall and the two columns of the pronaos were removed and replaced by an apse. At the same time the timber roof, normal in Greek temples, was replaced by the barrel-vaulting which still survives.

Scanty remains of painting, dating from the period of use as a church, can be seen on the north external wall.

When King Otto entered the new capital of Greece in 1834, a solemn service was held in St George's Church (depicted in a painting by Peter von Hess in the Neue Pinakothek, Munich). Thereafter it became a museum and continued to serve that purpose into the present century.

Metroon

The remains of the Metroon, a sanctuary of the Mother of the Gods (Meter Theon) built in the second half of the 2nd c. BC, lie in front of the Bouleuterion, on the west side of the Agora. Although the plan of the structure is difficult to distinguish on the ground, it consisted of four rooms with a colonnade on the east side to unify the façade facing on to the square. In the 5th c. the Metroon was converted into a Christian church, to which the mosaic pavement still visible on the site belonged.

Bouleuterion

The Bouleuterion, meeting-place of the Council (Boule) of Athens, was built in 403 BC on the slope below the Temple of Hephaistos. A vestibule on the south side led into the main council chamber, with the semicircular rows of seats for the 500 members of the Council rising in tiers like the auditorium of a theatre. The building was destroyed by the Herulians in AD 267, but was rebuilt and remained in existence until about 400.

Peribolos of
Eponymous
Heroes

Opposite the Metroon (see above) is a long narrow rectangular base. On this there stood statues of the ten eponymous heroes who gave their names to the ten tribes (phylai) into which the population of Attica was divided. Here in ancient times new laws were made public.

Altar of Zeus
Agoraios

Opposite the Metroon and a few paces east of the Peribolos of the Eponymous Heroes is an altar of Pentelic marble which originally stood on the Pnyx and was later moved to its present site. It is thought to have been dedicated to Zeus as patron of the Agora (Zeus Agoraios).

The oak and laurel trees flanking the altar were planted in 1954 by King Paul and Queen Frederica.

Statue of Hadrian

Among the numerous monuments the bases of which have been preserved along the west side of the Agora was a statue of the Emperor Hadrian (117–138) erected in the 2nd c. AD. This well-preserved figure is notable for the quality of the carving, particularly the richly decorated breastplate.

Temple of Apollo
Patroos

At the west end of the Agora, between the Metroon and the Stoa of Zeus at the foot of the Agora Hill, are the foundations of the temple of Apollo Patroos, built in the 4th c. BC over the remains of buildings destroyed in the Persian Wars and dedicated to Apollo as the father of Ion and thus the forefather of the Ionians. The cult image of Apollo and Euphranor from the temple is now in the Stoas of Attalos. In an annexe to the temple the earliest register of the population of Athens was kept.

Immediately north are the foundations of a small sanctuary of Zeus Phratrios and Athena Phratria, also dating from the 4th c. BC.

The north-west part of the Agora, extending to the Piraeus railway line (the construction of which destroyed its north end), is occupied by the Stoa of Zeus Eleutherios (Zeus who maintains the freedom of the city). This was built in the 5th c. BC, in a style reminiscent of Mnesikles' Propylaia on the Acropolis. It had projecting wings at each end, and in front of it, on a round base, stood a statue of Zeus Eleutherios. During the Roman period two rooms were built on to the rear of the stoa, probably for the purposes of the Imperial cult. Pausanias tells us that the Stoa of Zeus contained pictures, including representations of the Twelve Gods, Theseus and the battle of Mantineia.

Stoa of Zeus Eleutherios

The earlier belief that the Stoa of Zeus was the same as the Royal Stoa (see below) has been shown by recent excavations to be erroneous.

It was long thought that the Royal Stoa (Stoa Basileios) was identical with the Stoa of Zeus (see above), but it has now been located in the new excavation area north of the Piraeus railway. It is dated by the excavations to the mid-6th c. BC. It was destroyed in the Persian attack of 470 BC but was rebuilt soon afterwards. In the 4th c. BC this stoa, like its larger neighbour, the Stoa of Zeus, was extended by the addition of wings on either side.

Royal Stoa

The Royal Stoa was the seat of the Archon Basileus, who took over the cultic functions of the earlier kings. Among these functions was the trial of offenders accused of asebeia (impiety, godlessness); and accordingly this stoa may have been the scene of Socrates' trial in 399 BC, when he was condemned to death by drinking hemlock, after defending himself against charges of impiety and the corruption of youth in the "Apology" recorded by Plato.

The Altar of the Twelve gods dates from the time of the Peisistratids. In later times it enjoyed the right of asylum, affording sanctuary from pursuit. It was regarded as the central point of Athens, and distances from the city were measured from here.

Altar of Twelve Gods

The remains suffered damage during the construction of the Piraeus railway, and only one corner of the original structure now survives.

The Temple of Ares stood in the northern part of the Agora; originally built on another site around 440 BC, it was moved to its present position in the Augustan period. Although only scanty remains have survived, there is sufficient evidence to establish that this temple resembled the Temple of Hephaistos and was probably built by the same architect. The cult image of Ares, god of war, carved by Alkamenes, has been lost, but the excavators found a statue of Athena and a number of relief figures (from an interior frieze) which are now in the Agora Museum (see entry). Also in the museum is the central acroterion from the east front, representing Ares's sister Hebe.

Temple of Ares

Outside the east front of the temple is the Ares altar.

The state prison of Athens has recently been identified by the American archaeologist E. Vanderpool in the new excavation area to the south-west of the Agora.

Prison

Going south-east from the Tholos for some 100 m alongside the Great Drain, we see on the far side of a bridge (to the left of the drain) a substantial building (37.5 by 16.5 m – 123 by 54 ft) which is dated to the mid 5th c. BC. This has an open passage down the middle, with spacious cells on either side. The first two rooms on the right of the entrance, which communicate with one another, agree with Plato's description (in the

"Crito" and "Phaedo") of the prison in which Socrates spent his last days in the company of his pupils and finally drank the fatal dose of hemlock.

Eleusinion

On the east side of the Panathenaic Way (see page 59), which climbed up to the Acropolis, was a sanctuary of the Eleusinian divinities Demeter, Persephone and Triptolemos. It was smaller than the one in Eleusis, but large enough to accommodate a meeting of the Council of 500 on the day after the celebration of the mysteries.

In the centre of the precinct are the foundations of a temple, with an antechamber leading into the adyton (the "not to be entered" holy of holies). The temple, which stood on a high terrace, was extended south-ward in Roman times.

★Amphiáreion

Excursion
45 km (28 mi.) N

Bus (orange)
from
Mavromateon 29,
Ares Park

Open Tue.–Sun.
8.30am–4pm

The ancient sanctuary of Amphiaraos is beautifully situated in a quiet wooded valley in northern Attica, on the road from the little port of Skála Oropoú to Kálamos and Kapandríti (6 km (4 mi.)) south-east of Skála Oropoú.

Amphiaraos was a mythical king of Argos who possessed the gift of clairvoyance. On his way to Boeotia during the expedition of the Seven against Thebes he was victorious in a contest at Nemea during the funeral ceremony of the young prince Opheltes. During the battle for Thebes he was snatched away by Zeus and disappeared into a cleft in the earth. At this spot, on the borders of Attica and Boeotia, where he later re-emerged a sanctuary was established at a sacred spring where he was revered as a seer and as a hero who brought salvation and healing.

The mythical king Amphiaraos was worshipped in the Amphiáreion

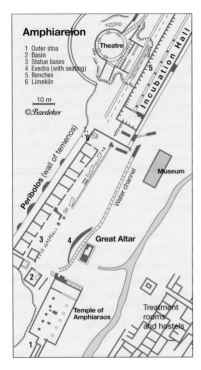

Amphiareion

1 Outer stoa
2 Basin
3 Statue bases
4 Exedra (with seating)
5 Benches
6 Limekiln

10 m
©Baedeker

Theatre
Incubation Hall
Peribolos (wall of temenos)
Water channel
Museum
Great Altar
Temple of Amphiaraos
Treatment rooms and hostels

The sanctuary and the cult of Amphiaraos have much in common with the Asklepieion at Epidauros (see entry). The site was excavated by Leonardos and Petrakos.

A path runs downhill from the entrance to the site, and immediately on the right is the **temple** (4th or 3rd c. BC). This had six Doric columns along the front between antae (pilasters).

The interior is divided into three aisles by two rows of five columns. A porch built on to the rear of the temple contained a second door leading to the priests' quarters. Against the rear wall of the cella can be seen the base for the cult image; in the centre is a table for offerings.

In front of the temple, beside the sacred spring, is the broad **altar**, which according to Pausanias was dedicated to Amphiaraos and numerous other divinities.

Archaeological site

Further along, beyond some statue bases of the Roman period (on left), is the **incubation hall** in which worshippers seeking a cure slept. The hall, which dates from the 4th c. BC, is divided into two aisles by a row of 17 Ionic columns, with 41 Doric columns along the exterior. Along the rear wall are stone benches. The two corner rooms were probably intended for women.

Behind the incubation hall is the **theatre**, with five marble seats of honour around the orchestra and a well-preserved stage building. The auditorium is overgrown with pines. In this theatre musical contests were held every five years from 332 BC onwards.

Further down are the remains of **Roman baths**. On the other side of the little stream are a klepsydra (water-clock) and the remains of houses.

The small **museum** contains interesting local finds.

Anaphiotiká K/L 7

Above the Pláka (see entry), most conveniently reached from the upper end of Erechthéos Street, is this little settlement, established by incomers from the island of Anaphí who came here in the 19th c. and built their little village-style houses on an area of undeveloped land below the Acropolis. Their church of St Simeon, built in 1847, is a plain aisleless structure.

Location
Pláka

Areopagos   K 7

Location
NW of the
Acropolis

North-west of the Acropolis (see entry) is the Areopagos (Areios pagos, Hill of Ares or Mars), seat of the supreme court of ancient Athens. There are three ways of reaching it.

Electric Railway
Theseion station

On the south side 16 rock-cut steps (smooth and slippery) lead up to a small plateau surrounded on three sides by further steps leading to the top of the hill.

Bus
230 (Apostólou
Pavlu)

From the Leofóros Dionysíou Areopagítou, some 150 m to the left (west) of the broad road leading up to the Acropolis, a path runs up in a north-westerly direction through an ancient residential quarter to the foot of the west side of the Areopagos.

Another footpath starts from the Leofóros Apostólou Pávlou, near the south-west end of the Agora (see entry) enclosure, and ascends the easy slope of the hillside, past numerous rock cuttings marking the sites of ancient buildings.

History The origins of the Areopagos go back to mythology. Here, according to tradition, Ares was called to account by the gods for the murder of Halirrhotios; and here, too, in Mycenaean times, as Aeschylus relates in his "Eumenides", Orestes stood trial for the murder of his mother Klytaimnestra. The goddess Athena herself secured his aquittal: whereupon the Erinnyes or Furies who had been relentlessly pursuing him – and who had a cave sanctuary on the Areopagos – turned into the Eumenides of "Kindly Ones". The event was commemorated by an altar dedicated to Athena Areia by Orestes, to which Pausanias refers.

A block of stone on the east side of the hill may have been this altar; or alternatively it may have been one of the two stones, the Stone of Wrath and the Stone of Shame, on which the accuser and the accused person sat at trials in historical times. In the 5th c. BC the power of the Areopagos was reduced to the role of a constitutional court and a court of morals.

Chapter 17 of the Acts of the Apostles records the address which the Apostle Paul gave to the "men of Athens" on this ancient sacred site, referring to Christ as the "unknown god" whom they worshipped. A modern bronze tablet (to the right of the steps up the hill) is inscribed with this text.

Church of
Dionysios the
Areopagite

On the northern slopes of the Areopagos are the remains of a basilica of the Byzantine period dedicated to Dionysios, a member of the Areopagos who – as recorded in the Acts of the Apostles – was one of Paul's first converts (see General, Quotations), and subsequently became the patron saint of Athens.

Residential
quarter

To the south-west of the Areopagos, below Leofóros Apostólou Pávlou, an ancient residential quarter has been excavated. On this site, now much overgrown, can be seen a street lined by the remains of substantial buildings (some of them with mosaic floors) and the sanctuary of the old local healing god Amynos, identifiable by its trapezoid plan.

In the northern part of the site is the assembly hall of the Iobakchoi, a Dionysiac fraternity. Inside is a marble pillar with bas-reliefs

Ares Park   L/M 5

Ares Park (**Pedion Áreos**) is an extensive park situated a little to the north-west of the National Archaeological Museum (see entry). On the edge of it is the large Mavromateon bus station, from where coaches leave for destinations in Attica. The main path through the park is lined with busts of Greek heroes. There is also an imposing memorial to Commonwealth soldiers who fell during the Second World War.

The park boasts some welcoming cafés and restaurants, with buskers here and there.

Just to the west of Ares Park lies Platia Viktorías (Victory Square), a pleasant place to rest under shady trees, with open-air cafés or small taverns.

Trolleybuses
2, 3, 4, 5, 7, 11,
12, 13 (Pedion
Áreos)

Bus
234 (Pedion
Áreos)

Platia Viktorías

Attic Riviera • Coast of Apollo

The coastline along the Saronic Gulf between Athens and Cape Soúnion is often called the "Attic Riviera" or the "Coast of Apollo". There were several villages here in ancient times, for example the sites of Áyios Kósmas or Anaphlystos near present-day Anávyssos, which have yielded some important finds. In more recent times, however, the area was only sparsely populated. It was not until the influx of Greek refugees from Asia Minor in 1922 that more settlements started up. The south coast of Attica experienced its greatest boom with the beginnings of mass tourism after the Second World War. A number of popular seaside resorts have sprung up: Páleo Fáliro, Kalamáki, Ellinikó, Glyfáda, Voúla, Kavoúri, Vouliagméni, Várkitsa, Lagonssi, Anávyssos, Legrená and Soúnion (see entry).

Location
10–70 km
(6–43 mi.)
south-east

Town buses
(blue-white)
from Syntagma to
Várkiza
Regional buses
(orange) from
Mavromateon,
Ares Park to
Soúnion

Glyfáda

Glyfáda is the largest resort on the Attic coast. Well-tended beaches with good facilities, such as Astir Beach, flourishing gardens and parks, efficient hotels, ultra-modern shopping streets and a wide range of leisure facilities – for example, an 18-hole golf course, four marinas and a yachting club – attract Athenians seeking a rest from their busy town and many other visitors. The resort is, however, badly affected by traffic from the major airport at Ellinikó nearby.

Location
19 km (12 mi.)
south-east

Buses
A3 from
Syntagma Square

Páleo Fáliro

At the southern end of the Syngrú arterial road lies the densely populated suburb of Páleo Fáliro, a seaside resort south of Athens that is steeped in tradition. It boasts the Flisvos Marina, one of the largest yachting harbours on the Attic Riviera, which is also the departure point for excursion boats and cruises to Aegina, Hydra, Póros and other islands in the Saronic Gulf and the Aegean.

In the north of the village are the **Hippodrome** (horse races Mon., Wed., Sat. 2.30pm), the **Planetarium** and the **Eugenides Institute** where physical experiments are demonstrated in a popular scientific way (open Mon.–Sat. 9.30am–1.30pm, Sun. 5.30–8.30pm).

In Trocadero Harbour, the old battleship **"Averof"** can be visited on Sundays. A veteran from the world wars, the Averof started active service in 1910 and at times served as headquarters of the Greek Navy. The Averof accompanied convoys through the Indian Ocean and, in 1944, it returned the exiled government to Greece.

The **Peace and Friendship Stadion**, completed after several years in 1985, is an ultra-modern utilitarian construction, designed by the Athenian architect Papagiannis. Situated on the beach promenade of Néa Fáliro, its daringly curved roofline can be seen from afar. The

Location
7 km (mi.)
south of the
town centre

Buses
(blue-white)
126, 149

oval stadium (measuring 87 × 43 m (285 × 51 ft) on the inside) has room for 16,000 spectators. A large number of additional offices are integrated into the building, for example for the care of sportsmen and –women, for training, administration and medical services. Major events of all kinds are held in the giant hall, for example sports contests, rock concerts, festivals and various exhibitions. The floor of the hall can be adapted to suit any event in a very short time.

★Vouliagméni

Location
23 km (14 mi.)
south-east

Buses
(blue-white)
A3 from
Syntagma

Vouliagméni, equally famous as a seaside resort and a thermal spa, is in a picturesque situation on the Attic coast. Even in ancient times the town was famous for the healing powers of its hot springs (24.6°C (76.3°F)) which feed into a greenish shimmering thermal lake. The water contains amongst other minerals sodium chloride, calcium chloride, magnesium sulphate and bicarbonate of magnesium, and it is effective in the treatment of rheumatic diseases, neuralgia, arthritis, skin diseases and women's complaints.

The fine, sandy beaches of Vouliagméni and surroundings are very busy, especially at weekends.

Ayía Dýnamis   L 7

Location
Mitropóleos
Street

Bus
025

The tiny aisleless **Church of the Holy Power** lies hidden below the modern block occupied by the Ministry of Education. It dates from the Turkish period and has a bell-cote built on to one side.

During the construction of the Ministry building remains of the Themistoclean Walls (see entry) were found. It is thought that one of the 15 gates in the walls, the Diochares Gate, stood near here (junction of Pentélis and Apóllonos Streets).

Ayía Ekateríni   L 8

Location
Lysikrátous Street

Trolleybuses
1, 5, 10, 12, 15
(Amalias)

St Catherine's Church, near Hadrian's Arch (see entry), dates from the 12th or 13th c., with later extensions, and has preserved its original dome and apses.

The church, reached by descending a short flight of steps, stands in a large courtyard planted with palms. In this garden are two columns of the Roman Imperial period; the function of the building to which they belonged is unknown, but it was probably part of an earlier church façade.

Ayii Anárgyri   K 7

Location
Erechthéos Street
(Pláka)

Bus
230

The 17th c. church of **SS Cosmas and Damianos** (with later alterations) in the higher part of the Pláka (see entry) belongs to the monastery of the Panayíou Táfou, a dependency of the Greek Orthodox Monastery of the Holy Sepulchre in Jerusalem. It is dedicated to the 3rd c. doctor saints Cosmas and Damian, the "moneyless saints".

The interior is in Baroque style, with a handsome throne and a carved and gilded iconostasis. In the courtyard are some fragments of ancient capitals.

Ayii Asómati   K 7

The little **Church of the Incorporeal Beings** stands in a little square in the lower part of Ermoú Street, at the junction with Asomáton and Lepeniótou Streets. It was built in the 11th c. and restored in the 20th c. Like many old buildings in Athens, it now lies below the present street level.

After the Greek war of liberation from the Turks, the church was converted to secular use and was occupied by a pharmacy.

Location
Ermoú Street

Electric Railway
Theseion station

Bus
025

★Ayii Theódori   L 7

The **Church of SS Theodore**, dedicated to the two military saints of that name, stands at the west end of Klafthmónos Square (see entry), near the University (see entry). Built in the mid 11th c. on the site of an earlier 9th c. church, it is very characteristic of its period: a domed cruciform church with a handsome ashlar exterior, with lines of brick between the courses of stone, a terracotta frieze of animal and plant ornament and Kufic script.

The bell-cote was added later and the interior is modern.

Location
Platia
Klafthmónos

Trolleybuses
1, 2, 4, 5, 11, 12,
15, 18

Ayios Dimítrios Lombardáris   K 8

This little church of **St Demetrius** stands in the gardens on the north-east side of the Hill of the Muses (see entry), on the right of the road which runs up to the parking place on the hill. It contains attractive wall paintings.

With its large courtyard, this is one of the churches most frequented by the people of Athens on the occasion of church festivals and processions.

Location
Apostólou Pávlou
Street

Electric Railway
Theseion station

Bus 230

Ayios Ioánnistin Kolóna   L 7

This little church of **St John of the Column**, standing in a small courtyard, takes its name from the Roman column in the chancel; the column has a Corinthian capital which projects through the roof.

John the Baptist, to whom the church is dedicated, is invoked for all diseases of the head and its organs. Attached to the column with wax are ex-votos in the form of threads, hairs and tablets.

Location
72 Evripídou
Street

Ayios Geórgios tu Vráchou   L 7

This tiny aisleless church (**St George of the Rock**), probably dating from the Frankish period, stands at the top of the stepped Epichármou Street, on the upper edge of the Pláka (see entry). It takes its name from its location immediately below the rock-face of the Acropolis. There is another church dedicated to St George on Lykabettos (see entry).

Ayios Ioánnis o Theológos   L 7

This beautiful 13th c. domed cruciform church (**St John the Evangelist**),

Location
W. of Pláka

71

with Roman capitals, stands in a little square at the intersection of Erechthéos and Erotokrítou Streets, in which a mulberry tree provides welcome shade.

Ayios Nikólaos Rangavá   L 7

Between the churches of Ayios Ioánnis o Teológos and Ayios Yeóryios tou Vráchou stands the 11th c. church of **St Nicholas**. It was attached to the palace of the Rangava family, which produced several Byzantine Emperors and Oecumenical Patriarchs.

Much altered in later centuries, the church was restored in the 20th c.

Ayios Nikodímos   M 7

Location
Filellínon Street

Trolleybuses
1, 5, 10, 12, 15
(Amalias)

The domed cruciform church of **St Nicodemus** is one of Athens' numerous 11th c. churches. Erected in 1045 (the date is recorded in an inscription), it was damaged by the Turks in 1780, purchased by the Tsar of Russia in 1845 and redecorated internally by the painter Ludwig Thiersch. Since then, re-dedicated to St Nicodemus, it has belonged to the Russian Orthodox Church. Immediately adjoining the church are ancient remains which, according to Travlos, belonged to baths attached to the Lykeion (Lyceum).

★★Benáki Museum   M 7

Location
Leofóros Vasilíssis
Sofías

Trolleybuses
3, 7, 8, 13 (L. Vass.
Sofías)

Buses
023, 234 (L. Vass.
Sofías)

Temporarily
closed

This museum is based on the rich private collections of Antonios Benáki, who lived in Cairo and collected Greek, Turkish and Chinese treasures.

Of particular interest is the Greek gold jewellery, mainly from Thessalia. Favourite motifs are Aphrodite and Eros, as well as the Knot of Heracles. There is an interesting collection of jewellery from the Byzantine and post-Byzantine period. Some pieces of jewellery and gold medallions appear to come from Venetian workshops. The silver cult-objects on display are mainly from Macedonia.

Mention should also be made of exhibits from Early Christian Egypt, especially the Coptic robes. There are a number of Byzantine and post-Byzantine icons, including a 14th c. representation of Abraham and a 15th c. picture of Demetrius, and one by El Greco (Domenikos Theotokopulos) depicting the Magi.

Also exhibited is ceramic work from Asia Minor.

Most impressive are Chinese vases and figures from the Tang dynasty.

Craftwork, including costumes and carvings, from several greek provinces are on display in the basement; there, too, is a copy of a reception room from the house of a nobleman in Koztni in the 18th c.

★Brauron

Excursion
33 km (20 mi.) E

Brauron (modern Greek **Vrávron** or **Vrávona**), on the east coast of Attica 8 km (5 mi.) north-east of Markópoulo, was of importance in ancient times for its sanctuary of Artemis. Excavated by Papadimitriou between 1948 and 1963 and excellently restored, it is now a most impressive and interesting site.

The Temple of Artemis at Brauron

The site of Brauron was occupied from the neolithic times. Remains of Middle Helladic buildings (2000–1600 BC) were found on the acropolis and there was evidence of dense settlement in the Late Helladic (Mycenaean) period (1600–1100 BC). After a period of abandonment the site was resettled in the 9th c. BC. Brauron's heyday was in the 5th and 4th c., but after 300 BC the land became waterlogged and was again abandoned. The cult of Artemis Brauronia was taken from Brauron to the Acropolis of Athens in the 6th c. by Peisistratos, a native of Brauron.

History In Mycenaean times the goddess Artemis was known here as Artemis Iphigeneia; and according to Euripides Iphigeneia, daughter of king Agamemnon of Mycenae, was a priestess at Brauron after her return from the Tauric Chersonesos until her death. During the Classical period Athenian girls aged between 5 and 10 served in the sanctuary. They were known as "little bears" (arktoi) from the saffron-coloured garments they wore, recalling a she-bear sacred to Artemis.

At the foot of a hill near the 12th c. chapel of St George (restored) is a small shrine, behind which are the **Cave of Iphigeneia** (now roofless) and a "sacred house".

To the north are the rock-cut footings of the **Temple of Artemis**, built in the first half of the 5th c. BC on the site of an earlier structure.

Lower down is a **courtyard** surrounded on three sides by colonnades, built between 430 and 420 BC. The entrance is on the west side, where there is an ancient stone bridge. The Doric columns of the colonnades, of limestone, had marble capitals. Six rooms in the north wing and three in the west wing each contained eleven wooden beds for the "little bears".

The **Museum** contains finds from the site: artefacts from the sanctuary of Artemis; pottery found on the acropolis, of Early to Late Helladic date (3rd millennium to 1100 BC); pottery from Anávyssos and the Peráti necropolis; and material from the Merénda necropolis (vases of the 9th–4th c. BC).

500 m inland are the excavated remains of an early Byzantine **church** (6th c.), a three-aisled basilica with a narthex and exonarthex. The east end, separated from the rest of the church by a screen, is closed by an apse, in which the semicircular seating for the officiating clergy (synthronon) can still be seen. At the east end of the south aisle is a small chapel, also with an apse. At the east end of this aisle is a doorway leading into the circular baptistery.

Buses (orange) from Mavromateon, Ares Park

Open Tue.–Sun. 8.30am–3pm
Admission fee

The basilica was evidently destroyed after a relatively short period of existence. Thereafter a small chapel, of which some remains survive, was built in the centre of the nave.

★Byzantine Museum   M/N 7

Location
Leofóros Vas.
Sofías

Bus
234 (L. Vas.
Sofías)

Trolleybuses
3, 7, 8, 13 (L. Vas.
Sofías)

Open Tue.–Sun.
8.30am–3pm

Admission fee

This valuable collection of Byzantine art from Greece and Asia Minor is housed in a palace built by Kleanthes in 1840, on a site which was then in open country, for the eccentric Duchesse de Plaisance, wife of Charles-François Lebrun, whom Napoleon made Duc de Plaisance (Piacenza).

In the courtyard are architectural fragments from Early Christian basilicas and Byzantine churches (5th–15th c.) and a reproduction of a fountain depicted in a mosaic at the monastery of Dafní (see entry).

The **left-hand wing** contains a large collection of icons.

Room 1: icons on the Life, Passion and Resurrection of Christ; the Trinity; Christ Pantocrator (Ruler of All); Life of the Mother of God; various saints.

Room 2: icons of the 16th and 17th c., including St Anthony, the Panayía Kardiótissa, St John the Evangelist and St Eleutherius. At one end of the room are an iconostasis and (to the right of this) a small tripartite altar. On the right-hand wall are the Life of the Mother of God and the Hospitality of Abraham.

Room 3: icons by Constantine and Emmanuel Tsanes.

Room 4: icons of the 17th and 18th c.

The **right-hand wing** contains late Byzantine and post-Byzantine icons (13th–16th c.).

There is a particularly interesting group opposite the entrance: a 12th c. icon of the Mother of God, with the version overpainted in the 17th c., which has recently been detached.

Main building The rooms on the ground floor illustrate the development of the church interior.

Room 1: A small-scale reconstruction of an early Christian basilica, with the templon, the screen which separates the chancel (**bema**), in which are the altar and the seats for the clergy (**synthronon**), from the rest of the church. Sculptured representations of the Good Shepherd, in which the old type of the lamb-carrier (see Acropolis Museum) is applied to Christ, and Orpheus.

Room 2: Byzantine reliefs, including a number of rare relief icons.

Room 3: A typical Middle Byzantine domed cruciform church (9th–11th c.), with a sculptured eagle on the floor marking the omphalos (navel).

Room 4: Example of a post-Byzantine church (17th–18th c.) with a carved and gilded iconostasis.

Individual items of particular interest:

The **upper floor** of the main building has numerous icons including some works of art from the post-Byzantine Cretan school.

Room 1: A mosaic icon of the Mother of God Episkepsis (145: 14th c.), Gospel books, historical documents (among them a chrysobull of the Emperor Andronikos II dated 1301).

Room 2: Gold jewellery from Lésbos.

Room 4: Liturgical utensils and vestments (particularly notable being a 14th c. epitaphios from Salonica – an embroidered pall used in the representation of the Holy Sepulchre on Good Friday); wall painting from Oropós.

Cemetery of Athens   M 8/9

The Cemetery of Athens

Location
Anapáfseos Street

Trolleybus
4 (Imitú)

Immediately south of the Olympieion (see entry) Anapáfseos Street (the "Street of Repose") branches off Ardíttou Street, a busy traffic artery, and runs up to the principal Athenian cemetery (**Próton Nekrotafíon Athinón**). After passing through the modern entrance hall we see on the left, near a chapel, the tombs of the archbishops of Athens. Then follows the imposing monument of George Averoff, who financed the construction of the modern Stadion and other buildings.

On the slope beyond this is the temple-style tomb of **Heinrich Schliemann**, designed by Ernst Ziller. The actual tomb has steps surrounded by reliefs. Above it, at the top of three steps, its base having reliefs depicting scenes from the Trojan War, stands a marble temple with Doric columns. On the west side is a bust of Schliemann.

Nearby is the tomb of **Admiral Kanáris** (1790–1877). On the left of the central avenue running down to the second chapel is the tomb of **Kolokotrónis** (1770–1843), one of the great heroes of the War of Independence.

★★Dafní

The monastery of Dafní, 10 km (6 mi.) west of the city centre, is famous for its 11th c. mosaics. The name recalls that this was the site of a sanctuary of Apollo, to whom the laurel (daphne) was sacred. The pagan shrine gave place to an early Christian monastery, which in 1080 was replaced by the present monastery, dedicated to the Dormition of the Mother of God (koimesis, kímisis), the Orthodox equivalent of the Assumption of the Virgin. In 1205, after the Frankish occupation of Athens, it was handed over to Cistercians from Burgundy and became the burial place of the Frankish lords (later dukes) of Athens. From this period date the battlemented defensive walls and a number of sarcophagi. At the beginning of the Turkish period the monastery was reoccupied by Orthodox monks. During the 19th c. war of liberation Dafní suffered damage and was abandoned. A thorough restoration in 1955–7 saved the buildings from further dilapidation. Both the church and the precinct wall were damaged by an earthquake in 1981.

Excursion
10 km (6 mi.) W

Bus
A16 (from
Eleftherias)

Open daily
8.30am–3pm,

Admission fee

Dafní

The monastery of Dafní is well-known for its mosaics

Dafní Church

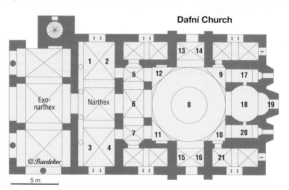

1 Betrayal
2 Last supper
3 Joachim and Anna
4 Presentation of the Virgin
5 Bacchus, Elpidophorus, Aphtonius, Pegasius
6 Dormition
7 Maradrius, Orestes, Auxentius, Sergius
8 Pantocrator and prophets
9 Annunciation
10 Nativity
11 Baptism of Christ
12 Transfiguration
13 Entry into Jerusalem, Nativity of the Virgin

14 Crucifixion
15 Incredulity of Thomas, Christ in the temple
16 Resurrection
17 Stephen, Silvester, Aaron, John the Baptist, Zacharias, Anthimus
18 Michael, Gabriel
19 Mary on the throne
20 Lawrence, Eleutherius, Gregory the Wonderworker, Nicholas, Gregory of Agrigento, Avercius
21 Magi

The picturesque and attractive courtyard of the monastery is bounded on the west by one side of the cloister, on the north by the south wall of the church and on the east by other monastic buildings. From the west entrance we pass through the Gothic exonarthex, dating from the period of Cistercian occupation, and the narthex into the **church**, which ranks with Osios Loukás near Delphi and the Néa Moní on Chíos as one of the three finest 11th c. Byzantine churches.

Mosaics The naos, on a Greek cross plan, is dominated by the large central dome from which the grave and majestic mosaic of Christ Pantocrator looks down. In the pendentives under the dome are four of the major themes of Orthodox iconography – the Annunciation, Nativity, Baptism of Christ and Transfiguration.

Of the numerous other mosaics the following are particularly notable: Raising of Lazarus, Entry into Jerusalem, Nativity of the Virgin and Crucifixion (north arm of cross); The Magi, The Risen Christ, the Presentation in the Temple and the Doubting of Thomas (south arm of cross); Mary between the Archangels Michael and Gabriel (chancel); saints (prothesis and diakonikon); Dormition (above door of naos); Prayer of Joachim and Anne, Presentation of the Virgin (narthex).

All these scenes show 11th c. mosaic art at its peak, in a fascinating blend of the Greek sense of beauty and Christian spiritualism.

The adjoining Tourist Pavilion is the scene of an annual Wine Festival (Jul.–Sep.), with free wine-tasting. Greek culinary specialities, music and dancing.

Dexameni Square   M 7

Dexameni Square (**Platía Dexaminis**), situated above Kolonáki Square at the foot of Lykabettos (see entry), is named after an ancient reservoir associated with an aqueduct constructed by the Emperor Hadrian (2nd c.). The aqueduct was brought back into use in the 19th c. The reservoir – now a small public garden – was embellished with an Ionic propylon, largely destroyed in the 15th c., of which a few fragments survive.

Bus (blue-white)
023 (Dexamenís)

Dionysios the Areopagite   L 8

Like the basilica on the northern slopes of the Areopagos (see entry), Roman Catholic **cathedral** is dedicated to Dionysios the Areopagite (St Denis). Built in 1853–87, it was designed by Leo von Klenze (1784–1864) and later re-designed by the Greek architect Kaftanzoglou. The basilica is fronted by a Corinthian arcade.

Location
Panepistimíou

Buses 024, 230

Trolleybuses
1, 2, 3, 4, 5, 7, 11, 12

Dionysius

Situated at an altitude of 460 m (1510 ft) on the north side of Pentélikon (see entry), on the road from Drosiá to Néa Mákri, is the village of Dionysius, one of the most popular places of resort around Athens. On the outskirts of the village is a sanctuary of Dionysos, which belonged to the ancient city of Ikaria, home of Thespis, who produced the first tragedy in Athens in 534 BC The introduction of vine-growing was attributed to King Ikarios.

Excursion
22 km (14 mi.) N

Buses
from Thission

Ermou   K 7–M 7

Location
Sýntagma
Square–
Kerameikos

Bus
025 (Ermou)

The Ermou axial road running east to west (Odós Ermú; Hermes Road) was laid when Athens was extended after 1834. It links Sýntagma Square with the main road to Piraeus, which it joins near the Kerameikos Cemetery (see entry). It is also the city's main shopping street, with the more expensive shops dominating the top part and small shops and workshops in the lower section.

The churches of Kapnikaréa and Ayii Asómati are worth a visit (see entries).

At the top end of the Ermou Evangelistrias and Ayíou Markou streets have recently been made into a pedestrian zone.

Fokionos Négri

Location
Patissíon–Kipseli

Trolleybuses
3, 5, 11, 12, 13
(Patissíon)

About 500 m north of Ares Park (see entry) Odós Fokionos Négri branches off in a north-easterly direction from the main Patissíon through-road. In recent years it has been made into an attractive pedestrian zone dotted with trees and fountains. A wide range of goods is on sale in numerous boutiques and small shops, and there are many restaurants and cafés.

Folk Art Museum   L 7

Location
Kidathinéon 17
(Pláka)

Open Tue.–Sun.
10am–2pm

The Greek Folk Art Museum in the Pláka is well worth a visit to obtain an insight into the traditions of Greek textile manufacture, including spinning and weaving, gold and silversmith work and wood carving. In a separate department artistically worked old and court robes are exhibited, some set with precious stones.

In a side room are some murals by the naïve artist Theophilos Hadzimihali (see also Hadzimihali House), who painted them at the end of the last century.

The ceramic department is housed in the Tzistarakis mosque on Monastiráki Square.

Gennadiós Library   N 7

Location
Suidias 61

Bus (blue-white)
023 (Suidias)

This library, assembled by a former Greek ambassador in London, Gennadiós, and donated by him to the American School of Classical Studies in 1923, is housed in a neo-classical building erected by the Carnegie Foundation. It is a specialised library on Greece, with more than 50,000 volumes in many different languages. (Open Mon., Wed., Fri. 9am–5pm, Tue., Thu. 9am– 8pm, Sat. 9am–2pm.)

Hadrian's Arch   L 8

Location
Leofóros Amalías

Buses
024, 230 (Amalías)

Trolleybuses
1, 15, 18
(Amalías)

To the west of the Olympieion (see entry), immediately adjoining the Leofóros Amalías, one of Athens' busiest traffic arteries, is Hadrian's Arch, erected in AD 131–132, when the gigantic temple of Olympian Zeus was finally completed. It is thought to occupy the position of an earlier city gate of the 6th c. BC, and was later incorporated by the Turks in the circuit of walls with which they surrounded the town in 1778 and which was pierced by seven gates.

The arch is a plain structure of Pentelic marble, bearing two inscriptions: on the west side, facing the Acropolis. "This is the ancient city of Theseus", and on the east side, facing the Olympieion, "This is the city of Hadrian and not of Theseus".

Hadrian's Library   L 7

Parallel to the Roman Agora (see entry) nearby is another complex of similar character but different function – the Library of Hadrian, founded by the emperor of that name after AD 132. This was a colonnaded court with exedrae (semicircular recesses) in the external walls. The entrance was on the west side, and part of this, richly decorated with Corinthian columns and a four-column propylon, has been preserved. It faces on to Areos Street, which runs south from Monastiráki Square past the old Sindriváni Mosque (now housing the Museum of Ceramics).

Situation
Eólou Street

Buses
10, 72

Temporarily
closed

The central room in the east range of buildings, much of which is still standing, was the actual library, and the niches in which the book rolls were kept can still be recognised. The building as a whole was not designed, like the Roman Agora, for business purposes, and the spacious courtyard was laid out as a garden, with a pool in the middle. The columns and other architectural fragments now to be seen in the courtyard came from the Megáli Panayía church, which was built in the 5th c. on the site of the original pool.

Hill of the Muses   K 8

The Hill of the Muses (Mouseion) is part of a chain of low hills to the south-west of the Acropolis, the others being the Pnyx and the Hill of the Nymphs (see entries). From the top of the hill (147 m – 482 ft) there is the classic and beautiful view of the Acropolis, with Lykabettos rearing up behind (see entries).

Bus
230

Trolleybuses
1, 5 (Draku)

From Dionysíou Areopagítou Street, at the point where it joins Apostólou Pávlou Street, a road branches off and goes up to a parking place on the far side of the hill. From here a path runs east along the rocky hill to the prominent monument of Philopappos, a prince of Commagene (south-east Anatolia) who was banished to Athens by the Romans and died there in AD 116. In gratitude for his munificence the Athenians allowed his ostentatious tomb to be erected on this exceptional site – an honour, it has been remarked, that was not granted even to a man like Pericles in the great days of Athens. On the frieze around the base Philopappos is shown in the guise of a roman consul, mounted in a chariot and accompanied by lictors. Above this are seated figures of the dead man and (to the left) Antiochos IV, his grandfather.

Philopappos
Monument

On the way to this monument are remains of the Diateichisma, the intermediate wall built in 337 BC to shorten the defensive lines between the Long Walls. Here too are various cisterns and rock-cut chambers, one of them traditionally misnamed the Prison of Socrates (now identified to the south-west of the Agora – see entry).

Diateichisma

Hill of the Nymphs   K 8

At the western end of the chain of hills which runs south-west of the Acropolis is the Hill of the Nymphs (Lófos Nimfón), easily identifiable by the domed Observatory on the summit. It is reached by way of a side street off Apostólou Pávlou Street.

Location
SW of the
Acropolis

Bus
230

The classical-style Observatory was built by Theophil Hansen in 1843–6 to the design of Schaubert. To the right of the entrance are the remains of the ancient sanctuary of the Nymphs from which the hill takes its name – a levelled rock surface and a dedicatory inscription. This level platform on the highest point of the hill was chosen by Ferdinand Stademann in 1835 as the viewpoint from which to draw his "Panorama of Athens".

To the south-east the Hill of the Nymphs merges into the Pnyx (see entry). From both hills there are fine views of Athens.

Hýdra

Area of island: 50 sq. km (19 sq. mi.)
Altitude; 0–590 m (0–1936 ft)
Population: 2800
Chief town: Hýdra

Ferries

There are scheduled ferry trips, lasting three and a half hours via Aegina and Poras, to and from Piraeus, hydrofoils from Athens (Zéa; one and a quarter hours), and local links with Spetses and Ermioni. There are also day cruises from Páleon Fáliron to Hýdra, Póros and Aegina.

The **island** of Hýdra (Idra, Saronic Island), known as Hydrea in ancient times, a bare, monolithic ridge of limestone off the south-east coast of Argolis (Peloponnese), is 12 km (8 mi.) long by 5 km (3 mi.) wide. This parched and infertile island survives mainly on tourism and local crafts, such as jewellery, ceramics, embroidery, handwoven fabrics and leather goods.

The picturesque town of Hýdra and its harbour

The local almond cakes (*amygdalotá*) – are to be recommended.

History Although there were settlers on the island as far back as Mycenaean times it remained relatively unimportant until the 18th c. In the 15th c. and again in 1770, after the Morean revolt, Albanian refugees came to Hýdra and – through trade, seafaring and, in particular, piracy – made it a culturally and socially rich centre. During the Greek struggle for independence from Turkey Hýdra converted its trading ships into a battle fleet and also bore a large share of the costs of the war. Today the island is once again of little commercial importance.

Sights

The island capital of Hýdra is picturesquely situated around the little sheltered harbour in the bay at the foot of the hills on the north coast. It boasts a merchant navy school and is a meeting-place of numerous painters and intellectuals. Near the quay stands the church of the former 17th c. monastery of Panayía, with its beautiful cloisters. On each side of the harbour basin can be seen the bleak early 19th c. residences of rich shipping and trading families, including those of Admiral Iákovos Tombázis (now a branch of the Athens Academy of Art), and of Demétrios Vúlgaris. The simple middle-class town houses, Cycladic in style but many brightly coloured, form a backcloth against the hills. To the west above the town lie the ruins of the medieval castle, including fortifications dating from the War of Independence.

Town of Hýdra

West of Hýdra, near the fishing village of Vlychós, lie the remains of the ancient town of Chorisa.

Surroundings

1½km (1 mi.) south is **Kaló Pigádi**, with a fine view and some 18th c. country houses round about.

To the south, charmingly situated in the mountains, stands the 15th c. monastery of **Profiti Elías** (the Prophet Elijah). The walk takes about three hours, or mules can be hired.

On the eastern tip of the island – also three hours on foot, mules available – is the 16th c. monastery of Zúrvas. There are also a number of other, mostly abandoned monasteries.

Dokós

To the north-west of the island of Hýdra lies the small pastoral island of Dokós, once known as Aperopia, with a village of the same name in a sheltered bay on the north coast.

Kaisarianí Monastery

The monastery of Kaisarianí lies beyond the eastern suburb of Kaisarianí, which is named after it, and is reached on a road that continues up to the monastery of Astéri (16th c. domed cruciform church, with frescos), then on to to the plateau of Hymettos (1027 m (3370 ft); military area, closed to public).

Location
7 km (4 mi.) E

The name comes from a spring close to a sanctuary of Aphrodite from which the emperor Hadrian caused an aqueduct to be built to supply Athens: thereafter the spring was known as kaisariane, Imperial. It was (and is) credited with healing powers, particularly for women who desire to bear a child. The water still flows from an ancient ram's head in the courtyard of the monastery.

Bus (blue-white)
224

Open Tue.–Sun.
8.30am–3pm

The monastic **church** is of the domed cruciform type. It was erected about the year 1000 on the site of an earlier church, and is thus rather older than the buildings of this type in Athens itself. The dome is borne not on the walls but on four columns with Ionic capitals, giving the

Kaisarianí Monastery: An oasis of calm

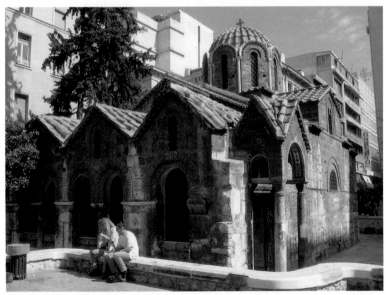

Kapnikaréa Church

interior an air of lightness. A templon formed of marble screens separates the chancel (bema) from the rest of the church.

The painting is much later than the church itself, having been done in the 16th c., during the Turkish period, probably by a monk from Athos. It is in strict accordance with the rules for the hierarchical disposition of the various subjects - Christ Pantocrator in the dome, with the Prophets round the windows and the four Evangelists in the pendentives; the Mother of God enthroned in the apse, with angels, the Communion of the Apostles and the fathers of the church below her; and on the barrel-vaulting of the arms of the cross the various church festivals. The figures stand out vividly against a black ground. In the porch is a fine representation of the Trinity. The porch, like the south chapel dedicated to St Antony and the bell-cote, was added in the late 17th c.

There are well-preserved remains of the **conventual buildings**. Entering by the main entrance, on the east side, we see on the left a building that was originally a bath-house (on the Roman plan, with hot, cold and warm baths) and later housed oil-presses. Beyond this, set back a little, are a twostorey range of cells and a tower house belonging to the Venizelos family of Athens, who were great benefactors of the monastery. In the right-hand corner are the kitchen and refectory (now a museum).

On the hill outside the west gateway of the monastery, beside the monks' cemetery (15 min. walk), are remains of churches dating back to the 6th c. From here there are extensive views of Athens.

Early Christian
churches

Kanellópoulos Museum   L 7

The important private collection assembled by Paul and Alexandra Kanellópoulos and now belonging to the state is housed in a neo-classical mansion on the upper edge of the Pláka, near the Metamórfosis church (see entries). It is of interest for its displays of both ancient and Christian art.

Location
Corner of Pánou
and Theorías
Streets (Pláka)

Basement: Icons, including the very beautiful wonder-working icon of the Panayía Myrtidiotissa (1747), a rare iconographic type.

Electric Railway
Monastiráki

Ground floor: Icons, liturgical utensils, silver and gold jewellery, embroidery; Egyptian mummy portraits and a painted death mask, a head of the Emperor Galerius (4th c. AD) and Byzantine coins (pre-1200).

Bus
(blue-white)
025 (Monastiráki)

First floor: Antiquities, including Greek pottery from the Geometric period onwards; pottery and metalwork from Cyprus; small marble Cycladic idols and stone implements and utensils of the Cycladic culture (3rd c. BC); Egyptian items in wood and metal.

Open Tue.–Sun.
8.30am–3pm,

Admission fee

Second floor: Pottery from Cyprus, Asia Minor, Cornith and Crete; Attic pottery (e.g. a vase with Priam, Hector and Andromache), a head of Alexander and Tanagra figurines.

Kapnikaréa Church   L 7

In a little square, opening off Ermoú Street, stands this interesting church, now the University church, which was saved from destruction during the construction of Ermoú Street in the 19th c. only by the intervention of King Ludwig I of Bavaria.

The Kapnikaréa is a very fine example of a domed cruciform church of the 11th c., with the little chapel of St Barbara on the north side. In the 12th c. a narthex with four pediments (originally open) was built on to the west end, giving architectural unity to the church and chapel. The graceful entrance portico appears to date from the same period.

Location
Ermoú Street

Bus
025 (Ermoú)

The paintings in the interior (19th c.) cover the complete iconographic programme as developed in the Middle Byzantine period.

Kerameikos   K 7

Location
Ermoú Street

Electric Railway
Theseion station

Bus
025 (Kerameikos, Ermú)

Open Tue.–Sun.
8.30am–3pm

Admission fee

Kerameikos, the potters' quarter of ancient Athens, was named after Keramos, the patron of potters, and has, appropriately given its name to the art and craft of ceramics. It was bounded on the north-west by the Agora and extended westward as far as the Academy (see entries). After 479 BC, when, following the Persian invasion. Themistocles enclosed the city within walls, part of the area lay within the walls and part outside them.

From the 12th c. onwards this area, on both banks of the Eridanos brook, was used for burial, and a continuous sequence of tombs can be traced from sub-Mycenaean times to late antiquity. The monumental funerary amphoras ("Dipylon vases") of the 8th c. BC, which can be regarded as the starting point of Attic funerary art, are now in the National Archaeological Museum (see entry), and the remains visible on the site are predominantly of the 5th and 4th c. BC The tombs are of many different types – individual tombs, funerary precincts, terraces of tombs – represented either by the originals or by copies. A plan is displayed to the north of the Museum.

This is the most thoroughly excavated of the cemeteries of Athens, by Greek archaeologists from 1863, by German archaeologists from 1913. Only part of the old Kerameikos quarter has been excavated – the area lying in the angle between Ermoú and Pireós Streets, beside the Ayía Triáda church. The residential area beyond the town walls, between the Sacred Gate and Ermoú Street, is at present under excavation. The whole site, still little affected by mass tourism, is quiet and full of atmosphere, although the surrounding area is not particularly attractive.

There are two gates through the walls at this point, the Dipylon and the Sacred Gate. The walls themselves were built by Themistocles in 479 BC and were strengthened in the 4th c. BC by the construction of outworks and moats. The more northerly of the two gates, and the one of greater architectural consequence, is the Dipylon.

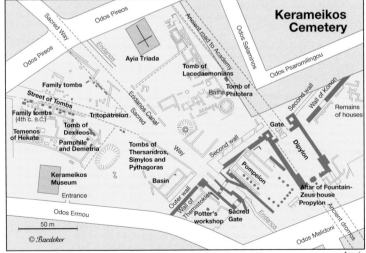

50 m

© Baedeker

84

"Street of Tombs" in Kerameikos

The cemetery area is traversed by three roads – the road to the Academy, to the N; the Sacred Way, further south, which ran from the Dipylon to Eleusis (see entry); and the Street of Tombs, which branched westward off the Sacred Way in the direction of Piraeus. All three of these roads are lined with tombs.

Going north from the entrance (past the Museum) on an ancient road, we pass on the left the tomb of two sisters, Demetria and Pamphile (c. 350 BC), and come to the **Street of Tombs**, with burials of the 5th and 4th c. BC (mostly 4th c.). Turning west (left) along this road, we pass on the left the equestrian monument of Dexileos (original in museum: see below), the tomb of Agathon and Sosikrates of Herakleia in Pontos (with three stelae) and the tomb of Dionysios of Kollytos, topped by a bull. Beyond this is the burial plot of Archon Lysimachides of Acharnai, built of polygonal blocks, guarded by a Molossian hound and decorated with reliefs (Charon, a funeral meal), and beyond this again is a crudely constructed altar belonging to a cult precinct of Hekate.

Returning along the same road, we see on the left two interesting family burial plots – the first belonging to the family of Eubios (stele of Bion) and the other to the family of Koroibos; this has a funerary stele in the middle, a relief of Hegeso (cast: c. 410 BC original in National Archaeological Museum – see entry) on the left and a loutrophoros (a large water jar for the bridal bath, set over the tomb of a person who died unmarried) on the right. Then follows (just before a side street on the left) a large round tumulus of the 6th c. BC belonging to one of the great families of the period. To the west, beyond the Eridanos, are the remains of another circular tomb, perhaps a heroon. Also on the left of the road is the small trapezoid sanctuary of the Tritopatores (ancestor gods), with inscribed boundary stones at the north-east and south-east corners. Beyond this, on the right, are the simple tombs of envoys from Kerkyra (c. 375 BC) and of Pythagoras of Selymbria (c. 450 BC) and a walled triangular cult precinct of unknown dedication. On the hillside behind is an aqueduct. The Street of Tombs now runs into the Sacred Way.

The **Sacred Way**, which leaves Athens by way of the Sacred Gate, is so called because it was the route followed by the solemn procession from the city to the sanctuary of the mysteries at Eleusis (see entry). To the north-west are the tombs of Antidosis and Aristomache and beyond these the handsome loutrophoros of Olympichos. In the other direction, towards the city, on the left the Sacred Way runs alongside the Eridanos to the Sacred Gate, and on the other side, opposite the ambassadorial monuments, are more graves, including a large round edifice, the tomb of an old Attic family.

The **Sacred Gate**, through which the procession to Eleusis left the city, is in the south-east part of the excavation site. There are two gateways. One of these spans the Eridanos on vaulting which is still preserved, and to the right

A sphinx from 550 BC in the Kerameikos Museum

of this is the main carriage-way. The road leads along the city wall (394 BC) north-wards to the Dipylon. On the left is the proteichisma, protected by ditches. The walls and ditches were first built at the end of the 5th c. BC, but the fine rectangular wall we see today dates from the end of the 4th *c.* BC

The **Dipylon** is the largest of the city gates of ancient Athens. As its name indi-cates, it is double, with a rectangular court between the two gates. Inside the inner gate are an altar dedi-cated to Zeus, Hermes and Akamas (son of Theseus) and a fountain-house.

Between the walls, the Sacred Gate and the Dipylon is the Gymnasion on the Eridanos, usually known as the **Pompeion** – the starting point of the procession (pompe) which made its way during the Panathenaic festival (Agora (see entry), Panathenaic Way) from here across the Agora to the Acropolis. There are remains of two build-ings, one overlying the other. The earlier one, dating from about 400 BC, consisted of a court surrounded by colonnades (6×13 columns): i.e., it was a gymnasion. Objects used in the Panathenaic procession were kept here. Wheel-ruts in the propylon show that the court was entered by wheeled vehicles. The rooms on the north side were probably the scene of the ceremonial banquet at the end of the festival; and it has been suggested (by Hoepfner) that the Panathenaic vases which were the prizes for victors in the contests may have been presented here.

This earlier building was destroyed by Sulla in 86 BC, and much later, in the 2nd c. AD, replaced by a three-aisled hall, which in turn was destroyed by the Herulians in AD 267.

The ground plans of the two overlapping buildings can be understood most clearly from outside the site, in Melidóni Street (turn left along Ermoú Street when leaving the site and then immediately left again).

On either side of the Dipylon two horos (boundary) stones set against the town walls mark the breadth (39 m – 128 ft) of the **road** which runs from here to the Academy (see entry). Along this road men who had fallen in war were buried in common graves, which were regarded with special honour. It was on one such occasion, at the beginning of the Peloponnesian War (431 BC), that Pericles gave the famous funeral ora-tion which is recorded by Thucydides. None of these graves of special honour has yet been found, but excavation has brought to light, at the second boundary stone on the south side of the road, the state tomb of the Lacedaemonians – the Spartan officers who died in 403 BC in the fight against the Thirty Tyrants of Athens.

Just on the edge of the excavated area are the remains of another (anonymous) tomb. Pausanias refers to other tombs of special honour on the road to the Academy, including that of Harmodios and Aristogeiton, murderers of the tyrant Hipparchos.

The museum, at the entrance to the site, contains the more recent finds; older finds are in the National Archaeological Museum (see entry). The musuem is notable for the large collection of pottery, illustrating both the history of the Kerameikos area and the development of Greek pottery types.

Kerameikos
Museum

The first room contains sculpture from tombs. Above the entrance doorway is a fragment from the Tomb of the Lacedaemonians (with the names of two fallen polemarchs in a script running from right to left). Immediately to the right of the entrance is the stele of Ampharete, showing the dead woman with her infant grandchild (c. 410 BC), and opposite this are a bronze cauldron (5th c. BC), an equestrian relief of Dexileos, killed in a skirmish at Corinth in 394 BC, and the stele of Eupheros (430 BC). Here, too, are a series of items of the Archaic period, including a seated figure with remains of colouring (530 BC) on the left-hand wall; a poros stele (570–560 BC) and a statue base carved with an equestrian procession (550 BC) in the centre of the room; and on the window side of the room another base with a wild boar fighting a lion (520–510 BC) and a sphinx (550 BC), the original colouring of which is shown in a reconstruction drawing on the wall. On the rear wall is the figure of a horseman (520 BC), and in the passage leading to the pottery collection is the head of a contestant in the pentathlon (560–550 BC).

Outside the museum, to the north, is a collection of modest funerary colonnettes (kioniskoi) – simple monuments set up after a sumptuary law of 317 BC banning the lavish tombs which had reflected 400 years of development of Athenian funerary art.

To the left of the entrance to the museum is a low hill which affords an excellent view of the whole site.

Kifissiá

The villa suburb of Kifissiá, situated at an altitude of 276 m (880 ft), is popular with both Athenians and visitors on account of its pleasant climate. In 1979 the remains of a large Roman bath-house of the 2nd c. AD were found here – probably belonging to a summer villa described by Aulus Gellius, the property of Herodes Atticus, a portrait bust of whom was found here in 1961 together with a bust of his pupil Polydeukes. In the square, under a protective roof, are a number of sarcophagi decorated with garlands which date from the same (Roman) period.

Excursion
15 km (9 mi.) N

Electric Railway
Kifissiá station

Buses
A7 (Kaminger)
550 (Stadion)

See entry.

National History
Museum

Klafthmónos Square   L 7

The south-west side of this square (**Platía Klafthmónos**), with the church of Ayii Theódori (see entry), borders the older part of the town (see Pláka). Along with the National Library, the University and the Academy, with which it is linked by Korai Street, it forms part of the replanned Athens of the first part of the 19th c.

Location
between Omónia
Square and
Sýntagma Square

In antiquity the boundary of the city ran through this area, and a section of the Themistoclean town walls of 479 BC can be seen in the square and at 6–8 Dragatsaníou Street (on the north-west side of the square).

Trolleybuses
1, 2, 3, 4, 5, 7, 9,
11, 12, 13, 15, 18

King Otto and Queen Amalia lived from 1836 to 1842 in a modest mansion (see below) at the south corner of the square, next to the only surviving classical-style building.

The first Greek Ministry of Finance also stood in the square, and its name (klafthmon, lamentation) refers to the complaints by government officials over the non-payment of their salaries.

The former King Otto Museum occupies a modest mansion, built in 1834, in which King Otto and Queen Amalia resided from 1836 until 1842, when they moved into the newly built palace in Sýntagma Square. The last descendant of the original builder (Stamatios

Museum of
Athens

Open Mon., Wed.,
Fri. 9am–1.30pm

Vouros), Lambros Evtaxias, had it restored to its original form by the architect Jannis Travlos, using the plans of its original German architects, Láders and Hoffer, and made it available to house the museum.

On the ground floor visitors can see the old kitchen. On the first floor are the apartments used by the royal couple, with their Empire and Biedermeier furniture – the Queen's room, the drawing-room, the King's study, the audience chamber, the room of the gentleman-in-waiting, the dining-room. In addition to numerous mementoes and pictures of King Otto's time (1815–67, reigned 1833–62), including loans from the Bavarian State Collections, the museum contains an interesting model of Athens in 1842, on a scale of 1:1000. Various views of the city and some architectural drawings complete the collection.

Kolonáki Square   M/N 7

Bus
023 (Kolonáki)

Trolleybuses
3, 7, 8, 13
(L. Vas. Sofías)

This square, situated in the embassy quarter between Leofóros Vassilíssis Sofías and Lykabettos, was for long a favoured residential district. In the gardens in the centre stands the small column from which it takes its name, and all round are the cafés and restaurants which make the square a popular place of resort for both young people and their seniors.

Vukurestíu

Vukurestíu, a narrow shopping-street, has recently been lovingly restored and pedestrianised. Some leading Greek jewellers and couturiers have established branches here, as well as some well-known foreign fashion houses.

Loútsa

Excursion
30 km (19 mi.) E

Buses
304, 305, 306, 316
(from Thission)

Behind the dunes at the coastal resort of Loútsa, 9 km (5½ mi.) east of Spáta and the same distance north of Brauron (see entry), a Doric temple of the 4th c. BC was discovered in 1956. It was probably dedicated to Artemis Tauropolos, for whom, according to Euripides, Orestes built a temple after returning from Tauris with his sister Iphigeneia and landing at Brauron. Loútsa is the ancient Halai Araphenides, where it is known from inscriptions that a festival of Dionysos was celebrated as well as the festival of Artemis, the Touropolia.

★Lykabettos   M 6/7–N 6/7

Bus
023 (Kleoménus)

Lykabettos, once well outside Athens but now surrounded by the city on all sides, is the dominant hill in the plain of Attica. It is a hill of cretaceous chalk, covered with various species of plant life, and is a popular place to go to escape from the hurly-burly of city life. At the top stands the chapel dedicated to St George, from where there are extensive views, especially to the south, to the Acropolis, Pnyx and Hill of the Nymphs (see entries), and over the Saronic Gulf.

Lykabettos Open-air theatre

To the north-east, down from the hill-top, is the Lykabettos open-air theatre, where both theatrical and musical performances, including rock concerts, are held.

Lysikrates, Monument of   L 7

The Monument of Lysikrates

The Monument of Lysikrates stands in a little square at the end of Lysikrátous Street. This rotunda, 2.80 m (9 ft) in diameter is surrounded by what appear to be pilasters but are in fact fully rounded Corinthian columns, between which curved marble slabs have been inserted. Round the top runs a frieze depicting scenes from the life of Dionysos (the transformation into dolphins of the pirates who had captured the god). The stone acanthus flower on the roof originally bore a bronze tripod, the prize received by Lysikrates when the choir which he had financed as choregos was victorious in the tragedy competition in 334 BC.

In 1669 the hollow monument was acquired by a Capuchin convent and used as a library, when it became known as the "Lantern of Diogenes".

This is the only surviving example of the numerous choregic monuments in the ancient Street of Tripods (which was on roughly the same line as the present street of that name). Other choregic monuments in Athens are the Monument of Nikias beside the Stoa of Eumenes (see Theatre of Dionysos) and the Monument of Thrasyllos above the Theatre of Dionysos.

Location
Lysikrátous and
Tripódon Streets

Bus
230 (Dionysíu
Areopagítu)

Trolleybuses
1, 2, 4, 5, 11, 12
(Amalías)

Metamórfosis   L 7

This little domed cruciform (**Church of the Transfiguration**) stands at the upper end of Klepsídras Street, which runs up from the Tower of the Winds (see entry) to a point immediately below the rock-face of the Acropolis. It can also be reached by taking the panoramic road (Theorías Street) which begins between the Propylaia (see Acropolis) and the Areopagos (see entry).

Although built in the 14th c., during the period of Frankish rule, the church is purely Greek in character. An early Christian capital serves as the altar of this modest place of worship.

Location
Theorías and
Klepsidras Streets
(Pláka)

Electric Railway
Monastiráki
station

Bus (blue-white)
025

Military Museum   N 7

The Military Museum, opened in 1975, is housed in a modern building between the Byzantine Museum (see entry) and the Hilton Hotel. The

Mitrópolis

Location
Leofóros Vas.
Sofías/Rizari

Trolleybuses
3, 7, 8, 13 (L. Vas.
Sofías)

Bus
234 (L. Vas.
Sofías)

Open Tue.–Fri.
9am–2pm,
Sat.–Sun.
9.30am–2pm

collection illustrates the story of the wars in which the Greeks have been involved, some of them of decisive importance for Greece itself (e.g. Navarino, 1827), others of major significance in world history (e.g. the Persian wars of the 5th c. BC), and emphasising the continuity of Greek history down the centuries.

The visit begins on the main floor. On one side of the long hall is a cast of the frieze of the Temple of Apollo at Bassai (original in British Museum). Here, too, are stone and bronze weapons of Neolithic and Mycenaean times, Corinthian helmets (5th c. BC) and material relating to the Battles of Marathon, Thermopylai and Salamis (490–480 BC). The other rooms continue in chronological order through the period of Alexander the Great, the Byzantine era, the periods of Frankish and Turkish rule, the War of Greek Independence and the fight for independence in Crete and Macedonia to the Second World War and Greek participation in the Korean war (1950–3). Some weapons and aircraft are displayed on the terrace.

Mitrópolis   L 7

Location
Platia Mitropóleos

Electric Railway
Monastiráki station

Bus
025
(Mitropóleos/Ermú)

In Mitrópolis Square, which is reached from Sýntagma Square (see entry) by way of Mitropóleos Street, are two churches of very different character – the medieval Little Mitrópolis and the modern Great Mitrópolis.

The **Great Mitrópolis** occupies the site of the monastery of St Nicholas which was destroyed in 1827. It is dedicated to the Annunciation (Evangelismós), which is represented above the main doorway, but is also known as St Nicholas in memory of the former monastery.

The church was built between 1842 and 1862 to the design of Schaubert, who set out to give the new capital of Greece a cathedral worthy of its status. The exterior displays the eclecticism of the 19th c., the interior leaning towards a rather sombre magnificence.

The Little Mitrópolis with the Great Mitrópolis behind

Beside the first pillar on the left is the tomb of Patriarch Gregory IV, who in 1821 was hanged by the Turks in Constantinople and is honoured as a neomartyr. (There is a statue of him in front of the University – see entry.) The principal festivals of the Greek Orthodox Church are celebrated in the Great Mitrópolis in the presence of the head of state.

The 12th c. **Little Mitrópolis**, a tiny domed cruciform church only 11 m (36 ft) long, is dedicated to the Panayía Gorgoepikoós (the Mother of God as the Swift Hearer of Prayer) and St Eleutherius, both of whom offer help to women in childbirth. This Christian church thus continues an ancient tradition, since the sanctuary of the Greek goddess Eileithyia, likewise the patroness of childbirth, was also located here. It is known as the Mitrópolis because it belonged to the monastery of St Nicholas, the residence of the metropolitans (archbishops) of Athens in the 18th and early 19th c. The monastery was destroyed in 1827, during the war of independence, and its site is now occupied by the Great Mitrópolis.

The church is unique in that it is not built of the usual dressed stone and brick but of fragments taken from ancient and medieval buildings. Above the entrance can be seen two parts of an ancient calendar frieze (arranged in the wrong order) with relief representations of the months, flanked by two pilaster capitals. Elsewhere are a variety of figural reliefs, including a figure of Cybele enthroned (in pediment on east side), fragments of funerary aediculae, etc. Many of the ancient fragments have been "Christianised" by having crosses carved on them. Compared with the fascination and charm of the exterior, the interior of the church, restored in the 20th c., is of little interest.

Monastiráki Square   L 7

In this square, named after the monastery to which the Pantánassa church belonged, all the different phases of the history of Athens are represented. In the middle of the square is the Pantánassa, a foundation dating back to the 10th c. At the south-east corner is one of the city's two surviving mosques, known as the Sindrivani after the former purification fountain, and which now houses the Ceramic collection of the Museum of Popular Art. Immediately behind the mosque, in Areos Street, is the pillared façade of Hadrian's Library (see entry) a monument of the

Location
NW edge of the
Pláka

Electric Railway
Monastiráki
station

Bus
025 (Monastiráki)

Monastiráki Square with its Electric Railway Station is a busy shopping area

Roman period; and further south is Athens of the Classical period, with the Acropolis (see entry). Finally there is the Electric Railway station to represent the modern age.

The square itself and the adjoining streets and lanes are a centre of busy commercial activity. To the north is Athinás Street, a busy thoroughfare that runs north to Omónia Square (see entry) through the bazaar-like market area. To the east is Pandrósou Street, with its numerous small shops selling icons and small antiques as well as souvenirs and jewellery. In the little streets to the west the flea market has been established; here one can buy every conceivable variety of second- and third-hand object. Here, too, in Adrianoú Street, are the shops specialising in copper ware.

Pantanassa
Church

The church of the Pantánassa (the Mother of God, Protectress of All), also known as the Panayía Megálou Monastíriou, is all that remains of the 10th c. nunnery which gives Monastiráki Square its name. It is a three-aisled basilica, with three columns between the aisles and an elliptical dome over the central aisle. The interior is richly decorated but of little artistic interest.

Moníton Klistón

Excursion
25 km (16 mi.) NW

Bus (orange)
260 From Liossion
to Filí

Going north-west from the village of Filí (or Chassiá) in the direction of ancient Phyle (see entry), we come in 4 km (2½ mi.) to Moní ton Klistón, the **Convent of the Gorges** (on right). After passing a large modern school building we reach this small well-preserved nunnery, perched on the rim of the deep gorge of the River Gouras. The 14th c. domed cruciform church is dedicated to the Dormition of the Mother of God (Kímisis tis Theotókou).

From the courtyard there is a cableway over the gorge to a spot marked with a white cross on the vertical rock-face opposite, where, according to tradition, an icon was found which led to the establishment of the nunnery. The cableway is used to take burning candles across to this inaccessible spot.

Higher up the gorge was a cave sacred to the shepherd god Pan, the setting of Menander's comedy "Dyskolos".

Museum of Cycladic Art   M 7

Location
Neofytu Duka 4

Trolleybuses
3, 7, 8, 13
(L. Vas. Sofías)

Bus
234
(L. Vas. Sofías)

Open Mon.,
Wed.–Fri.
10am–4pm,
Sat. 10am–3pm

Admission fee

The Museum of Cycladic Art in the Kolonáki quarter of the city was opened in 1986. It is housed in an attractive building donated by the N. P. Goulandris Trust. The ship-owner Nikolas P. Goulandris became well-known as a patron of cultural life in Athens, and it is his own collections of Cycladic and ancient Greek art that form the backbone of the exhibitions here. Some of the works of art on display are more than 5000 years old.

On the **ground floor** will be found Cycladic exhibits going back to between 3200 and 2000 BC, the oldest being some stout terracotta jugs. Small figures, delicate marble statuettes, grave-goods, idols in animal and human form, and other objects in clay, bronze, marble and obsidian complete the picture.

Greek works of art from between 2000 BC and AD 600 are displayed on the **upper floor**, earth colours dominating on the walls and in the glass display cases. Note especially the richly decorated vases and dishes, including a "kottabeion" from the 5th c. BC and a collection of twenty objects worked in bronze, as well as some interesting items in marble, glass and gold.

★★National Archaeological Museum   L 6

The National Archaeological Museum in Patission Street built by Ludwig Lange in 1860 and since then considerably enlarged, contains the largest collection of Greek art in the world.

Repeated visits are necessary to get anything approaching a complete idea of the wealth of its collections. Here it is possible just to draw attention to a selection of the most notable exhibits.

Room 4 Mycenaean art. Material excavated by Schliemann and others at Mycenae and other Mycenaean sites, illustrating the richness of the Mycenaean culture, which combined the nobility and monumentality of Achaean Greek art with the refinement of Minoan Crete (1600–1150 BC).

The exhibits are not arranged chronologically but according to sites or types of material. The front part of the hall is occupied by material from Mycenae itself, including the famous gold mask of a king from Shaft Grave V (c. 1580 BC), together with gold cups, vases, carved ivories, richly decorated daggers, boar's-tusk helmets, the "Warrior Vase" (c. 1200) and two pilasters from the entrance to the "Treasury of Atreus".

Particularly notable items in the rear part of the hall are the two famous gold cups from Vaphió, south of Sparta, which date from the 15th c. BC.

Room 6 Cycladic art. Material of the 3rd and 2nd millennia BC from the Cyclades. Characteristic of the highly developed art of this insular culture are the "Cycladic idols" and "Cycladic pans", ritual objects associated with the cult of the dead and of the gods.

Notable items are the Harp-Player from Keros (one of the few preserved male Cycladic idols) and the flying-fish frescoes from Phylakopi on the island of Milos (5844: 16th c. BC).

Returning to the entrance hall, we continue clockwise through the chronologically arranged collections, beginning with the Geometric period (9th–8th c. BC) and continuing through the Archaic (7th–6th c.) and Classical (5th–4th c.) to the Hellenistic (3rd–1st c.) and Roman periods.

Room 7 Archaic art. In the centre is the Dipylon Vase from the Kerameikos cemetery, a monumental sepulchral vase in Geometric style with a representation of the lament for the dead, dating from the time of Homer (c. 750 BC).

On the right-hand wall is a flat, almost board-like, relief from the island of Delos, dedicated by Nikandre (c. 650 BC).

Metopes from the Archaic temple of Athena at Mycenae (c. 620 BC).

Room 8 Archaic art. Two kouroi from Soúnion dominate this room some 3 m (10 ft) high 625–600 BC). When Greek artists began to produce large sculpture after 650 BC they achieved monumental expression in over-life-size figures of naked youths (kouroi). Characteristic of these figures are the rigidly frontal pose and the equal distribution of weight on both legs, with the left foot always in front of the right. Originally the hands were held close to the thighs, with clenched fists; later the arms hung free.

Also in this room are the head and hand of a kouros from Kerameikos (the "Dipylon Head", c. 600 BC).

Room 9 Archaic art. Winged Nike (Victory) from Delos (c. 500 BC) and, to the right, a slender kouros from Milos (c. 550 BC). Of particular interest is the excellently preserved kore holding a lotus flower in her left hand, with an inscription giving her name as Phrasikleia (4889). This figure was found by Mastrokostas in 1972 at Merénda, near Markópoulo in Attica.

Location
Patission

Electric Railway
Viktoria

Trolleybuses
2, 3, 4, 5, 7, 8, 9, 11, 13, 14, 15, 18, 21

Open Mon.
12.30pm–6.45pm,
Tue.–Fri.
8am–6.45pm, Sat.,
Sun., pub. hols.
8.30am–2.45pm

Rooms 10, 10a Archaic art. The kouros in this room was also found at Merénda. Stylistic comparisons suggest that the figure of Phrasikleia (see Room 9) was carved about 540 BC by Aristion, a sculptor from Paros working in Attica who was also responsible for the figure of Kroisos from Anávyssos in Room 13. In Andrew Stewart's view the Merénda kouros and the Theseus and Antiope group from Eretria (Chalkis Museum) are also by Aristion or his school.

Also in this room is a fine ephebe with a discus from the Dipylon (c. 560 BC).

Rooms 11, 12 Archaic art. Stele of Aristion, by Aristokles (29: c. 510 BC); kouros from the island of Kea (c. 530 BC).

Relief of a running hoplite from Athens (c. 510 BC); heads from the east pediment of the Temple of Aphaia, Aegina.

Statue of Zeus

Room 13 Archaic art. More kouroi, including a late Archaic figure with arms akimbo from the Ptoion (c. 510 BC) and a powerful figure from Anávyssos by Aristion of Paros (c. 540 BC), with an inscription on the base: "Stop at his grave and weep for the dead Kroisos, destroyed by wrathful Ares while fighting among the warriors in the forefront of the battle."

Room 14 Archaic art. Classical art, includes a relief of Aphrodite from Milos (470–460 BC) and a relief of a youth with a garland (originally a metal attachment) from Soúnion (c. 470 BC).

Room 15 Eleusinian votive relief (on left) depicting Demeter giving the first ear of corn to the boy Triptolemos, with her daughter Persephone or Kore (c. 440 BC).

In the centre of the room is an imposing over-lifesize bronze statue of a god found in the sea off Cape Artemision (northern Euboea); it was previously identified as Poseidon but is now generally recognised as representing Zeus.

Room 16 Classical art. Funerary monuments, including a large marble lekythos from the tomb of Myrrhine (c. 420 BC).

Room 17 Classical art. Votive relief from Piraeus depicting Dionysos with actors (c. 400 BC); head of Hera from the Argive Heraion (c. 420 BC).

Rooms 19, 20 Classical art. Votive relief with figures of Demeter and Persephone (c. 420 BC); torso of Apollo of the "Kassel Apollo" type (Roman copy of a Greek original of the 5th c. BC); votive relief dedicated to Pan and the nymphs, from the south face of the Acropolis (410 BC); the "Varvakion statuette", a small Roman copy of Phidias' Athena Parthenos (128: 2nd–3rd c. AD).

Garden Room From 20 visitors can enter one of the inner courts of the Museum.

Room 18 Relief of Hegeso and her maid, the most famous of the Kerameikos monuments (c. 400 BC).

Room 21 The Diadumenos, a Roman marble copy of a lost bronze original by Polykleitos (c. 410 BC), and (straight ahead) the Hermes of Andros, a Roman copy of an original of the school of Praxiteles (4th c. BC) – two works which exemplify the change from the vigorous but controlled physical representations of the 5th c. to the spiritualised approach of the 4th. Also in this room is the boy rider (2nd c. BC), recently mounted on a horse that is well restored but is not his original mount.

Room 36 The Karapanos Collection, with numerous small bronzes of the Archaic and Classical periods, including a horseman from Dodona (*c.* 550 BC), a goddess with a dove (Aphrodite or Dione) from the Pindos (460 BC) and the famous statuette of Zeus hurling a thunderbolt from Dodona (450 BC).

Other notable items in this room are an Archaic head of Zeus from Olympia (*c.* 550 BC) and a number of pieces of sculpture from the Acropolis, including a male head with inlaid eyes (*c.* 490 BC), the head of a youth (*c.* 480 BC), also with inlaid eyes, and an Athena Promachos (*c.* 450 BC).

We now return to the main circuit.

Room 28 The Ephebe of Antikythera, an original work in bronze, probably representing Paris or Perseus and carved by Euphranor (340 BC).

Fresco of children boxing from Akrotíri on the island of Santoríni

At the end of the room are a figure of Hygieia, probably by Skopas (c. 360 BC) and a head of Asklepios from the island of Amorgos (4th c. BC).

Room 29 A large group from the sanctuary of Despina at Lykosoura (Peloponnese) and a large statue of Themis from Rhamnous (early 3rd c. BC).

Room 30 Poseidon of Milos (2nd *c.* BC); bronze heads of a boxer from Olympia (*c.* 350 BC), a philosopher (3rd *c.* BC) and a man from Delos (*c.* 100 BC).

Rooms 31 to 33 are dedicated to Greek sculpture in Roman times from 1st c. BC until AD 5th c.

Other collections housed in the National Archaeological Museum include an interesting Epigraphic Collection (entrance from Tossitsa 1: open Tue.–Sun. 8.30am–3pm; extra admission fee), and a fine

Epigraphic Collections

★National Gallery   N 7

The National gallery (Alexandros Soutsos Museum) is housed in a new building in Leofóros Vasiléos Konstantínou.

On the ground floor are icons and pictures by Greek painters of the 19th and 20th c. (historical and genre pictures, seascapes, portraits).

National Garden

Location
Leofóros Vas.
Konstantinou 50

Trolleybuses
3, 7, 8, 13
(L. Vas. Sofías)

Bus
234
(L. Vas. Sofías)

Open Mon.-Sat.
9am–3pm,
Sun., pub. hols.
10am–2pm,
closed Tue

On the upper floor are pictures by European painters, including Caravaggio, Tiepolo, Rembrandt, Breughel and Jordaens, and among the moderns Picasso, Braque and others. Works by the Cretan-born El Greco occupy a place of honour.

There are also works by many Greek painters, including Nikólaos Gizis, Nikifóros Lýstras, Andréas Kriézis, Vikéntios Lántsas and Simeon Savvídis. Visitors are likely to be particularly interested in their pictures on Greek subjects (scenes from the everyday life of the people, the ever popular theme of the Acropolis).

In the basement are a collection of graphic art and special exhibitions, as well as a cafeteria. The new sculpture gallery is also worth a visit.

National Garden   M 8

Location
Amalías

Trollybuses
2, 4, 11 (Olgas)

The National Garden (Ethnikós) was originally laid out by Queen Amalia, wife of King Otto, and together with the adjoining Záppion garden it was the only large open space in Athens until the area extending from the Agora to the Hill of the Muses (see entries) was laid out as a park in quite recent years.

Záppion

To the south of the National Garden are the gardens around the Záppion, an exhibition hall with a Corinthian portico and a semicircular colonnade to the rear built by Ernst Ziller for the Zappas brothers.

National Historical Museum   L 7

Location
Plateia
Konokotrónis,
Odnos Stadíou

Trolleybuses
1, 2, 4, 5, 9, 10,
11, 18
(Stadíu)

Open Tue.-Sun.
9am–1.30pm

Admission fee

The **Old Parliament** (Voulí), which now houses the very fine collections of the National Historical Museum, was built in 1858–74 to the design of a French architect, Boulanger. In front of its stands an equestrian statue of Theódoros Kolokotrónis, one of the heroes of the fight for Greek independence.

The entrance hall leads into a narrow **Hall of Honour**, with busts of king Otto and George I and busts and portraits of prominent figures in the fight for independence, as well as those of politicians (e.g. Ypsilántis, Miaoúlis, Kanáris, Kolokotrónis and a heroine of the struggle for independence, Bubulína). From this hall three doorways give access to the old Parliamentary chamber, in neo-classical style.

Room A Weapons, medals, paintings and other objects from the Byzantine period.

Room B Mementoes from the period of Turkish rule, including documents belonging to the secret society known as Philiki Etairia.

Rooms D–F Reminiscences of the heroes of the 1821 Revolution. Memorabilia belonging to the patriarch Gregorios V and Lord Byron, as well as the urn containing the ashes of Paul Bonaparte, a nephew of Napoleon.

Room H Pictures of the rebellion in Crete and uprising in Macedonia.

Room I Portraits of heroes and battle paintings from the period of the struggle for freedom from the Turks.

Room J Documents from the time of Kapodistrias, King Otto I and King George I.

The Old Parliament, now housing the National Historical Museum

Natural History Museum

The Natural History Museum (open Sat.–Sun. 9am–2pm) in the northern suburb of Kifissiá (see entry) provides an excellent insight into the animal and insect life of the Mediterranean countries.

It boasts a fine collection of butterflies and one of mussels, as well as numerous stuffed reptiles and mammals. The highlight of the museum is the 8 m (26 ft) long skeleton of a triceratops, a member of the dinosaur family. On sale at the museum shop articles in real silver, semi-precious stones and mussel-shells are good value.

Location
Levidu 13
(Kifissia)

Electric Railway
Kifissiá

New Palace   M 7/8

The New Palace (Néa Anáktora), on the east side of the National Garden (see entry), was built in 1890–8 by Ernst Ziller (who also designed Schliemann's house (see entry) and other buildings in Athens) as the Crown Prince's Palace. It became the royal palace in 1935 after the restoration of the monarchy, and since 1974, when Greece became a Republic, it has been the official residence of the President. In front of the palace Evzones in their traditional costumes mount guard.

Location
Iródou tou Attiloú

Bus 234
(L. Vas. Sofías)

Trolleybuses 2, 4,
11 (Stadion) 3, 7, 8,
13 (L. Vas. Sofías)

★Odeion of Herodes Atticus   L 8

The large complex of buildings on the south side of the Acropolis extends from the Theatre of Dionysios at the east end by way of the Stoa of Eumenes (see entry) to the youngest of the three structures, the Odeion of Herodes Atticus, at the west end. This is named after the wealthy and munificent Herodes Atticus of

Situation
Dionysiou
Areopagitou
Street

Bus
230 (Dionsíu
Areopagítu)

Marathon (AD 101–177), who built it after the death of his wife Regilla in 161.

Its proximity to the Theatre of Dionysos (see entry) provides a convenient demonstration of the difference between the Greek and Roman methods of theatre construction.

The **Greek theatre** fitted its auditorium into a natural hollow, and the rows of seating extended round more than a semicircle. The orchestra was originally exactly circular, as at Epidauros, and the low stage structure (skene) lay close to it on one side, only loosely connected with it. Between the auditorium and the stage were open passages for the entrance of the choir (parodoi).

The principles of **Roman theatre** construction, as exemplified in the Odeion of Herodes Atticus, were quite different. The auditorium (cavea) was exactly semicircular, the side entrances were vaulted over and the stage, which in the later period was increased in height, was backed by an elaborate stage wall (scenae frons) of several tiers, lavishly decked with columns and statues, which rose to the same height as the top rows of seats or the enclosure wall of the auditorium. The auditorium and the stage thus formed an architectural unity, and the theatre became a totally enclosed space. The theatre was open to the sky, but an odeion (odeon), intended for musical performances, would be roofed.

The 32 steep rows of seating in the Odeion of Herodes Atticus (restored with a facing of white marble) could accommodate an audience of 5000. The structure, which was incorporated in the defences of the medieval castle, is in such an excellent state of preservation that it is used during the Athens Festival every summer for dramatic performances and concerts by leading Greek and European artistes.

Parliament

Location
Sýntagma
Square, E side

Trolley buses
1, 2, 4, 5, 9, 10,
11, 12, 15, 18
(Sýntagma)

Buses
025, 040, 230
(Sýntagma)

Tomb of the Unknown Soldier

The Parliament **Old Palace**, a fine Classical building of 1834–8 on plans of the architect Friedrich von Gártner, dominates the east side of Sýntagma Square (see entry). The complex which served kings Otto I and George I is laid out around two inner courtyards. The Doric columns facing the square and the long south gallery with sixteen Doric portico facing the National Garden (see entry) survive from the original plans of Leo von Klenze.

In Sýntagma Square, beneath the west front of the building, lies the **Tomb of the Unknown Soldier**. At 11.15am every Sunday the changing of the guard takes place here by the Evzones in their traditional uniform. On the walls on each side of the tomb are bronze shields listing Greek victories in the battles following 1821.

Olympic Sports Centre

Some years ago a large sports centre was built north of Athens, and the 1991 Mediterranean Games were held there. Athens also had high hopes of being chosen as the venue for the 1996 Olympic Games, but lost out to Atlanta in Georgia, USA. An application was also submitted to host the Games in the year 2000.

Location
10 km (6 mi.) NE

Electric Railway
Irini

It is intended that the 100 ha (247 acre) site will house a large stadium, a sports hall, a swimming hall, a cycling stadium, a training centre and a sports academy.

The two-tiered Olympia Stadion, providing seating for some 80,000 spectators, was completed in 1982. Underneath the west grandstand are rooms for the athletes, offices for the management committee, medical facilities, media studios, administration and VIP lounges. Two smaller halls are available for the athletes to warm up in.

Olympieion   L/M 8

A temple to the supreme god of the Greek pantheon Zeus, who had previously been worshipped in the open air, was built by Peisistratos on this site at some time before 550 BC – a hundred years before the erection of the temple of Zeus at Olympia. It was rather smaller than the later Parthenon (see Acropolis). The site, to the south-east of the Acropolis, then lay outside the city.

Location
Leofóros Olgas

Trolleybuses
2, 4, 11
(Olgas)

Peisistratos' sons Hippias and Hipparchos resolved to replace this temple by a gigantic new structure with a double colonnade (dipteros), comparable with the temple of Hera built by Polykrates on the island of Sámos.

Open Tue.–Sun.
8.30am–3pm

Admission fee

History Work on this building was suspended after the expulsion of Hippias in 510 BC, and it lay unfinished until about 175 BC, when the Syrian king Antiochos IV commissioned a Roman architect, Cossutius, to complete it. The new temple was designed to have a double colonnade of Corinthian columns, some 17 m (56 ft) high, of Pentelic marble; but this temple, too, remained unfinished, and it was not completed for another 300 years, until about AD 130, when Hadrian had it finished in accordance with Cossutius' plan. Its construction had thus taken altogether 650 years.

Because it is a symbol of the time when Athens was oppressed by a Syrian king and a Roman emperor, the Temple of the Olympian Zeus – the largest temple in Greece – has always been something of a thorn in the flesh of the people of Attica. The Olympieion is still overshadowed by the Acropolis, although the quality of its construction deserves more attention.

Temple of
Olympian Zeus

The cella, which contained a statue of Hadrian as well as the cult image of Zeus, has disappeared, as have most of the 104 columns, the making of which used some 15,500 metric tons of marble. The remains, however – a group of 13 columns and part of the entablature at the south-east corner, two isolated columns on the south side, and another column that collapsed in 1852 – still retain something of their original grandeur. It is not certain whether the 13 south-east columns belong to the Hellenistic building and the three on the south side to the Roman one, or whether they are all of Roman date.

The entrance to the site is in Leofóros Olgas. Near the entrance in the

Olympia comes Home

Never again Olympia! All Greeks, and especially all Athenians, were agreed on that in 1990, after the International Olympic Committee had made its decision public: the Olympic Games of 1996 were to take place not in Athens, but in the American Atlanta. And Athens had been so certain: was there any town on Earth other than Athens which could claim the right to host the jubilee games, 100 years after the first Olympic Games of the modern day of 1896? It is possible, however, that it was exactly this certainty which bordered on arrogance – and of course the prospect of many millions of American dollars – which swayed the Olympic demi-gods of Lausanne to bypass Athens.

Perhaps it was sufficient for Athens to see that the Games of Atlanta indeed turned out to be the final triumph of Coca-Cola and commercialism that many had feared; in any case, the joy was enormous when, in September 1997, the Greek capital found that its bid to host the Olympic Games in the year 2004 had been accepted. Thus the Olympic Games of the modern day return to their birthplace, albeit a little late.

A return to the beginnings is also what the educationalist and historian Baron Pierre de Coubertin had in mind when, in 1894, he founded the International Olympic Committee. He was intent on reviving religious values with the help of the Games, for they had probably originated in the culture of the Ancient Greeks. To honour their gods, the Greeks held sports contests up and down the country, where the disciplines of chariot races, pancratium (ring and fist fights) and shot-putting attracted the largest audiences and lured with such irresistible prizes as a tripod (first prize) or an intelligent woman (second prize). The most important games were those of

Olympia, a main site of worship of the god father Zeus. These games are documented for the first time in 776 BC with lists of the winners; in the year AD 393 they seem to have ended when the Byzantine emperor Theodosius I forbade all pagan practices in his edict. By this time, however, fame and greed had long become a normal part of the athletes' lives, because a victory at Olympia bestowed honour and bought favours back home for the sportsmen, in some cases even a political career – as you can see, not much different from the present day.

Thus, many gave in to temptation and sportsmanship vanished. In a yet-to-be-written 'chronique scandaleuse' one could mention the fist fighter Kleomedes, for example, who, in 492 BC, felled his opponent with an illegal blow, was disqualified and subsequently went mad. Seventeen statues of Zeus at the entrance of the Olympic stadium, too, would find a mention here: Olympic winners, who had been convicted of fraud or bribery, had to erect such statues as a punishment. All this of course did not lessen the public enthusiasm for the athletes. A regular hero worship competed with the worship of the gods in the neighbouring temple; legends surrounded exceptional sportsmen, and their statues were said to have healing powers.

At least in the beginning, however, the worship of the gods was still in the foreground. Initially, there was only one sports discipline, the stadium race. The list of sporting disciplines was fixed only during the 25th Olympic Games when the four-horse chariot race was introduced. Before then, over the years, ring fighting, pentathlon (five disciplines) and fist fighting had been added. The course of the contest had long had a strict ritual character. Those who did not arrive on time, at least 30 days before the beginning of the games, or who did not prepare in seclusion for the subsequent celebrations, were not allowed to participate. The fact that the athletes competed in the nude is a further indication of the religious character. Artists, too, made use of the occasion and presented their

Athens' successful marketing campaign to host the Olympic Games in 2004

works to the public. Thus, in the course of time, besides the religious and sportive events, a literary and musical fringe programme developed. The numerous hymns which honour the winners, for example the Epinician Odes by Pindar, bear a musical witness of this.

The role that Olympia played in the political life of Greece also steadily increased. During the games, a truce was declared throughout the entire country, and even if there was no medals table yet, a victory brought much prestige for the athlete's home town. Permission to participate also settled any questions as to who was a Hellene and who was a barbarian. The Romans counted as the latter who had to conquer Greece first before being allowed to take part. Then they sent their celebrities, too, – the emperors

Tiberius and Nero both took part in the chariot races.

Baron de Coubertin probably did not expect that Kaiser Wilhelm or Tsar Nicholas would take part when, in 1896, he announced the first Olympic Games of the modern day. With his nose for historical occasions, however, he based them in Greece – although in Athens, rather than Olympia which lay in ruins. In ancient times, the Pan-Athenian games had taken place here, and the new games were to be held in the reconstructed stadium. The preparations, however, caused a serious government crisis in Greece which was already shaken by financial problems. The merchant Georgios Averoff saved the situation and donated approximately one million Drachmas for the reconstruction of the Pan-Athenian stadium for which, in the old tradition, the country thanked him with a marble statue. When in the subsequent contests a Greek named Spyros Louis managed to win the first Olympic marathon race in the history of the sport, national euphoria reached antique proportions.

Whether such successes can be repeated in the year 2004 – this time in the Olympic stadium 'Spyros Louis' built in 1982 – remains to be seen. In the last few decades, Greece's athletes have not made Olympic history. What the Athenians are expecting from Olympia is something much more pragmatic: the enlargement of their underground network and other measures to rescue the city centre from suffocation by traffic.

There is a more general question as to whether Olympia 2004 might not be taking place without the Athenians. If one considers the Athletics World Cup of 1997, which was supposed to be the crowning glory of the application campaign one has to have one's doubts: the World Athletics Association very thoughtfully planned them for the month of August. Then, however, with temperatures of almost 40°C, it is unbearable in Athens. The sportsmen had to appear, but the Athenians preferred to leave the town and go to the seaside. As we all know, the Olympic Games take place during the months of August and September.

The Temple of Olympian Zeus

old defensive ditch of Athens, are a number of column drums from the Peisistratid temple. Further west are the remains of Roman baths and other buildings. Through the partly reconstructed propylon we enter the large rectangular temenos in which the temple lies. From the south wall of the temenos we can look down into an excavated area on a lower level in which, among other structures, the foundations of the temple of Apollo Delphinios and the large rectangle of the Penhellenion can be distinguished. They are among the many temples and shrines on the banks of the Ilissos, which flows underground through this area; others include the temple of Aphrodite in the gardens on the right bank of the stream, the Metroon and the shrine of Artemis Agrotera on the left bank. In Christian times a basilica was built here by the ancient Kallirhoe spring; mosaics are in the Byzantine Museum. A footpath leads along the eastern external wall of the Olympieion.

Omónia Square   L 6

Location
N of City centre

Electric Railway
Omónia
Bus (blue-white)
024 (Omónia)

Trollybuses
1, 12 (Omónia)

Omónia Square (**Platia Omonías,** Square of Concord) and its immediate surroundings are one of the busiest parts of Athens – busy in terms of traffic, commerce and tourism, with numerous offices, shops and hotels. In the centre of the square are gardens and a fountain; but around it tall modern blocks have almost completely displaced the low classical buildings of the 19th c., creating a cosmopolitan atmosphere in sharp contrast to the male society of the typical old Greek coffee-houses.

Additional traffic and business is brought to the square by its Electric Railway station and underground shopping arcade. Omónia Square was laid out by the town-planners of the 19th c. It was originally intended to be the site of the new royal palace that was finally built in Sýntagma

Square (see Parliament). From this square radiate two sides of the isosceles triangle which was the basis of the city plan – Pierós Street to the south-west and two parallel streets, Panepistimíou and Stadíou Streets, to the south-east. The third side of the triangle is formed by Ermoú Street, which is bisected by Athinás Street, running south from Omónia Square. A third of the way down Athinás Street is Kótzia Square, with the Town Hall and the main post office.

400 m (1320 ft) south of Omónia Square is Athens **market hall** for meat.

Omorphi Ekklisía

The Omorphi Ekklisía (**Beautiful Church**) is a 12th c. domed cruci-form building that owes its name to its graceful proportions and its handsome exterior of carefully fitted dressed stone. In the 14th c. a chapel was built on to the south side and a painter of considerable quality, probably from Salonica, embellished the interior with fine frescoes.

Excursion
8 km (5 mi.) N of
City Centre

Electric Railway
Patissía station

Paenía

The village of **Liopési** occupies the site of ancient Paiania, the birthplace of Demosthenes (384 BC), and is thus also known as Paenía. It is now an agricultural centre. Its late Byzantine churches (Ayía Paraskeví, Ayía Triáda, etc.), with frescoes, are of a type found also at Markópoulo (10 km (6 mi.) south-east) and Korópi (6 km (4 mi.) south). The Kanakis taverna is popular with visitors from Athens.

Excursion
6 km (4 mi.)

Buses
303, 308, 310
(from Thíssion)

The Vorres Museum of Contemporary Art is located on an idyllic old farm in Peania, on the eastern side of the Hymettos mountain ridge. On display are paintings and sculptures by well-known Greek artists, together with a smaller exhibition which ranges from historic Byzantine icons up to works by modern Greek painters and some folk art.

Vorres Museum

Open Sat., Sun.,
pub. hols.
10am–2pm

A particular tourist attraction is the Koutoúki stalactitic cave on the east side of Hymettos (see entry), discovered in 1926, which can be reached from the village on an asphalted road. The cave, 500 m (1640 ft) above sea level, has an area of 3800 sq. m (40,000 sq. ft) and is indirectly lit.

Koutoúki cave

Open daily
9.30am–4.30pm

Párnis

This range of limestone mountains rising to 1413 m (4636 ft) divides Attica on the north from Bogotia. In ancient times there was a sanc-tuary of Zeus the Rain Bringer on the summit. Nowadays Mount Párnis attracts many visitors with its pine forests and its pleasant cli-mate.

It is reached by way of the outlying suburb of Achárnes (see entry), starting-point of a 12 km (7½ mi.) road that winds its way up with numer-ous sharp bends. After passing a sanatorium (alt. 1000 m – 3200 ft) the road comes in 2 km (1¼ mi.) to the Ayía Triáda chapel, where there are a tourist pavilion and a hotel.

Here the road divides: the right-hand branch leads to the Mount Parnes Casino and luxury hotel, while to the left (3 km – 2 mi.) is a mountain hut from which it is possible to climb to the summit.

Excursion
31 km (19 mi.)
NW

Bus
738 (Párnis)

Cableway

The Koutoúki stalactitic cave at Paenía

Pentélikon

Excursion
16 km (10 mi.) N
Buses 411, 415,
421, 422 (Pendéli)

The Pentélikon of Pendéli range (1109 m – 3639 ft) bounds the plain of Attica on the north-east. Pentelic marble was used in the great classical buildings on the Acropolis (see entry) and by the great sculptors of that time.

Pendéli
Monastery

Leaving Athens by way of Leofóros Kifissiás and going north-east, we pass through the suburb of Chalándri and come in another 8 km (5 mi.) to a village with a poplar-shaded square (restaurant) in which is Pendéli Monastery, founded in 1578 (alt. 430 m – 1410 ft). The monastery buildings are modern. In the basement, which is entered from outside, visitors are shown various sacred books and one of the "secret schools" in which monks taught children during the period of Turkish occupation.

A flight of steps to the right leads into the monastery courtyard with its beautiful little church and ranges of cells.

The road continues past the monastery to a square surrounded by cafés, where there is a small church set among trees. From here can be seen the marble quarries that disfigure the hill and the modern installations on the summit. Below the square, among the trees, is a little country house which belonged to the Duchesse de Plaisance; the house is now surrounded by modern bungalows (in Leofóros Dukíssis Plakentías).

Daou Pendéli
Monastery

On the eastern slopes of Pentélikon is another monastery, Daou Pendéli. It is reached by leaving Athens on the Marathón road and turning left 21 km (13 mi.) from the city centre. Daou Pendéli, founded in the 12th c. and rebuilt in the 16th, has been called "the only example of a large monastic establishment in Greece outside Athos" (Kirsten-Kraiker).

Phyle

Phyle (**Fili**), like Panakton (on the old road from Athens to Thebes) and Dekeleia (near present-day Tatói, on the east side of Mount Párnis), was one of a ring of frontier fortresses built in the 4th c. BC to protect Attica against attack from the Megarid and Boeotia to the west.

The road from Athens runs via Anó Liossía to the village of Filí (terminus of bus) and continues north-west past the Moní ton Klistón (4 km – 2½ mi.); see entry). 6 km (4 mi.) beyond the monastery, at the end of the asphalted road, the fortress of Phyle can be seen on the left.

Phyle stands in a rugged mountain setting on a rectangular plateau (alt. 638 m – 2241 ft), commanding the pass which carried the old road from Athens to Tanagra in Boeotia. The site had probably been occupied by an earlier fortress in which Thrasyboulos assembled his followers in 403 BC for the attack on the Thirty Tyrants. The west and south-west parts of the 4th c. fortress (excavated by Skias in 1900) have collapsed into the gorge.

Considerable stretches of the imposing walls of dressed stone have been preserved to the level of the wall-walk on the east and south-east.

Excursion
18 km (11 mi.)
NW

Bus (yellow)
260 (from Liossion)

★**Pireaus** (Pireéfs)　　　　　　A 10–12/E 10–12

Piraeus (modern Greek Pireás; pop. 250,000), which together with Athens forms a conurbation, is the largest port in Greece and the starting point of services to Europe and the Middle East and of most domestic services.

Excursion
9 km (5½ mi.) SW

Elektrikós Piraeus

History It was Themistocles who in 482 BC made Piraeus the commercial and naval port of Athens. The city was connected to Athens by the Long Walls (see Themistoclean Walls) and in the time of Pericles was laid out on the rectangular plan of Hippodamos of Miletus.

The town was destroyed by Sulla in 86 BC and thereafter was a place of no importance. In the Middle Ages it was known as Porto Leone after the two marble lions which flanked the entrance to the harbour. One of them now stands in front of the Arsenal in Venice.

Piraeus recovered its importance after the liberation of Greece in the 19th c., when the modern town was laid out on a rectangular plan (by Schaubert) as the ancient one had been.

Stations
Terminus of State and Peloponnese Railways

Port In addition to the principal harbour of Kantharos the two smaller ancient harbours on the east side of the town – Bassalimáni (the ancient Zea) and Mikrolímano, formerly called Turkolímano (the ancient Mounychia) – are still in use. New port installations to relieve the pressure on Piraeus are being developed in Pháliron Bay, site of the earliest harbour of Athens before the foundation of Piraeus.

The most characteristic parts of the modern town, which combines the atmosphere of a large port with the amenities of a city, are around the principal harbour, in Korais Square on the higher ground between that harbour and Mikrolímano with its numerous tavernas.

Ancient sites The remains of ancient boat sheds can be seen under water in the two harbours on the east side, and behind the Archaeological Museum in Chariláou Trikoúpi Street is a Hellenistic theatre (2nd c. BC). Stretches of Konon's town walls (394–339 BC) can be seen at the south-west tip of the town.

In the Archaeological Museum of Pireaus (Chariláou Trikoúpi 31; open Tue.–Sun. 9am–3pm) can be seen the famous bronze statues of Athene

Archaeological Museum

(4th c. BC) and Apollo (6th c. BC), which were rediscovered some time ago in the nearby harbour. Other exhibits include black and red figured vases, tomb reliefs and interesting representations of battles between Greeks and Amazons.

The Maritime Museum (open Tue.–Sat. 8.30am–2pm, Sun., pub. hols 9am–1pm) is housed in a modern semi-circular building on the Zea Marina, with the development of Greek sea-faring since ancient times being explained by exhibits covering twelve rooms. There are drawings and models of old ships as well as portrayals of famous sea-battles, including the battles of Salamis (see Salamis) and Lepanto.

Maritime Museum

★Pláka   L/M 7

The Pláka, the older part of modern Athens, lies between the northern slopes of the Acropolis (see entry) and Ermoú Street, extending east almost to the Leofóros Amalías. In its narrow streets and little

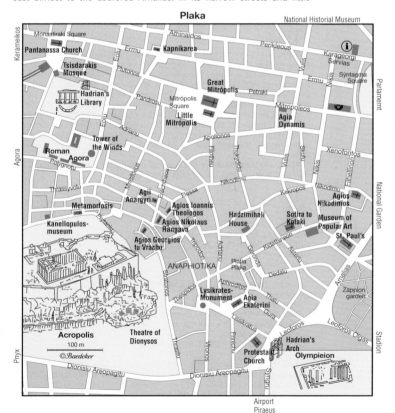

◀ *The Mikrolímano harbour in Pireaus*

107

Location
Town centre

Electric Railway
Monastiráki station
Buses 025
(Ermú/Mitropóleos)
230 (Amalias)

Trolleybuses
1, 5, 12, 13, 15, 18
(Amalías)

squares are a number of small churches, from the Metamórfosis (south-west – see entry) to the Sotír tou Kottáki (east), from Ayios Nikodímos (south-west – see entry) to the Kapnikaréa (north – see entry). It is a district of houses in neo-classical style, mostly of modest size, with attractive tiled roofs. At 5 Thólou Street is an old building (altered by Kleanthes) which housed the University (see entry) before its move to Christian Hansen's new building in Epistomíou Street. The building is now a taverna.

Since 1978 the city council have been introducing preservation orders on the Pláka area. Half of the buildings are listed as of historical or architectural importance, and any conversions and renovations are subject to strict regulations. Most streets are barred to traffic.

A pleasant evening **walk** can be taken from the Mitrópolis through the Filotheu and Adrianou or the Kidathineon, past the Platia Pláka to the Lysikrates Monument. Here are found souvenir stalls, rows of small shops selling sweets, dried fruits and nuts, leather-goods, jewellery and fashion clothes, and taverns with or without bouzouki music

Pnyx   K 7/8

Bus (blue-white)
230 (Apostólou
Pávlou)

The Pnyx (110 m – 361 ft) is one of the range of three hills – the others being the Hill of the Nymphs and the Hill of the Muses (see entries) – to the south-west of the Acropolis (see entry). After the reform of Kleisthenes (508–507 BC) the Ekklesia, the popular assembly of Athens, met here, before moving to the Theatre of Dionysos (see entry) in the 4th c. BC. Here men like Themistocles addressed the people of Athens. There are remains of the rock-cut orators' platform, with the altar of Zeus (c. 400 BC) behind it; the retaining wall (c. 330 BC), built of huge blocks of stone, which supported the semicircular auditorium on the north, and the diateichisma, the wall built in 337 BC to shorten the line of the city's defences.

Along the west side are the rows of seating for the spectators of the *son et lumière* shows which now take place here.

Póros

Area: 23 sq. km (9 sq. mi.)
Altitude: 0–345 m (0–1130 ft)
Population: 4000
Chief town: Póros

Ferries

Ships ply between the island and Piraeus 3 times a day, the trip taking two and a half hours.

Hydrofoils several times a day from Piraeus (Zéa), taking one hour.

Regular shuttle service to Galatas on the mainland.

Local links with the islands of Hýdra, Spétsae and Aegina and the Methana peninsula.

Day cruises from Páleo Fáliro to Hýdra, Póros and Aegina.

Póros (Saronic Island), the headquarters of the ancient Kalaurian League, and the ancient Kalaureia, lies to the south-west off the Methana (Peloponnese) peninsula and is separated from the north coast of the Argolid by a shallow strait (1 mi.) long up to 1 km (⅔ mi) wide and 1½ km. (1 mi.) Much of the island is covered in sparse woodland.

The **population**, some of Albanian extraction, live mainly from produce

A taverna in the Pláka

Póros is situated on a peninsular

grown along the fertile coastal strips on the mainland that belong to Póros, and from the increasing tourist trade.

History There was a town here in Mycenaean times, on the site of the later Sanctuary of Poseidon. The ancient city was abandoned in Roman times; the present town was established only in the late Middle Ages.

Sights

Póros town

The town of Póros (population 3900) is beautifully situated on the ancient Sphairia, the southernmost part, connected with the main part of the island by the narrow promontory of Bisti. In the 18th and 19th c. it was the main defensive harbour on the south-east coast of Greece.

Sanctuary of Poseidon

About 5 km (3 mi.) north-east of the town can be found slight traces of the 6th c. BC Sanctuary of Poseidon, which formed the nucleus of the "Kalaurian amphictyony" (cult association of tribes) of the seaside towns on the Saronic and Argolic Gulf. The temple enjoyed the right of sanctuary; and it was here that Demosthenes, the great advocate of resistance to the Macedonian hegemony, poisoned himself in 322 BC while fleeing from Antipatros. A number of ruined remains round and about indicate where the old town of Kalaureia lay.

Monastery of Zoodóichos Piyí

This 18th c. monastery lies some 4 km (2½ mi.) east of the town of Póros.

Troizén

10 km (6 mi.) to the west of it, near the village of Damalás, are slight remains of the ancient town of Troizén, the scene of the legend of Hippolytos and Phaidra.

Pórto Ráfti

Excursion
38 km (24 mi.) E, on the Attic coast

Bus (orange) from Mavromateon, Ares Park

Pórto Ráfti, a picturesque little port on the east coast of Attica, 9 km (6 mi.) south of Brauron (see entry), is named after a large marble Roman statue, popularly known as the "Tailor" (raftis), on a rocky islet outside the harbour.

The predecessor of the present town in ancient times was Prasai, on the hill of Koroni at the south-east end of the bay, which played an important part in the shipping trade between Attica and the islands during the 7th and 6th c. BC. The ancient town walls that can still be seen, however, date only from the 3rd c. BC.

To the north of Pórto Ráfti bay was **Steiria**, to which a Mycenaean necropolis in the Peráti district belonged (finds in Brauron museum).

Railway Museum   K 5

Location
Sioku 4

Open Fri.–Sun.
9am–1pm

In the Athens Railway Museum various locomotives and coaches can be admired. The oldest rolling stock in the museum dates from the second half of the 19th c., and includes some trains used by the Greek King George I and the Ottoman Sultan Abdul Aziz. A number of steam locomotives and trams have been lovingly restored, and old railway equipment and models complete the collection.

★Rhamnoús

The ancient coastal town of Rhamnoús is reached from the village of

The Temple of Nemesis in the ancient port of Rhamnóus

Marathón (see entry) by way of Káto Soúli. Coming from the south the road leads on to the terrace of the sanctuary of Themis and Nemesis, the goddesses of the legal order and of retribution.

Excursion
52 km (32 mi.) NE

This is a small Archaic **Temple of Themis**, a temple of grey limestone built around 500 BC and further embellished after the Persian wars. A cult figure by the sculptor Chairestratos (c. 280 BC) is in the National Archaeological Museum (see entry).

Buses (orange) from Mavromateon, Ares Park

Adjoining is the larger **Temple of Nemesis**, for which Phidias or his pupil Agorakritos carved the cult image (c. 420 BC: fragments in National Archaeological Museum, Room 17). It is a Doric peripteral temple, built in marble, with 6×12 columns, begun about 430 BC but – as can be seen from the unfinished state of some of the columns – never completed. In front of the temple is the altar.

Open Mon.–Sat. 7am–6pm
Sun. 8am–6pm

From the temple terrace there are beautiful views over the site of the ancient town, now largely overgrown with macchia.

A footpath flanked by tombs runs down to the sea, above which rises the hill on which the **Acropolis** was built. Remains of walls can be seen on the east side, and of a theatre on the seaward side.

★Roman Agora   L 7

The Roman Agora or Market was laid out at the beginning of the Christian era immediately west of the Tower of the Winds (see below), built some decades earlier. It was connected with the older Greek Agora to the west by a road which was discovered some years ago.

Location
Pelópida/Eólu

While the Greek Agora grew and developed over the centuries, this later market was laid out on a unified rectangular plan. It has two gates: at the west end a Doric propylon built between 12 and 2 BC with an inscription recording that the market was dedicated to Athena

Bus (blue and white) 025 (Monastiráki)

Open Tue.–Sun. 8.30am–3pm

Archegetes, and at the east end an Ionic propylon probably dating from the reign of Hadrian (AD 117–138), when the adjoining Library of Hadrian (see entry) was also built.

Probably dating from the same period are the colonnades of slender unfluted Ionic columns that surround the market, as well as the shops and offices that open off the colonnades. On the south side is a fountain.

The **Tower of the Winds** stands in the Pláka below the north side of the Acropolis (see entries). In the planning of the modern city of Athens in the 19th c. Eólou Street, named after the wind god Ailos, was aligned directly on the tower, which forms a landmark at its southern end.

Built in the 1st c. BC, the tower is an octagonal structure 12 m (40 ft) high, with sundials on the external walls; it originally housed a water-clock. Around the top runs a frieze with reliefs representing the eight wind gods – the beardless Notos, pouring out rain from an urn (south); Lips, holding the stern ornament of a ship (south-west); Zephyros, a youth scattering flowers (west); Sykron the bringer of snow (north-west); the bearded Boreas, blowing into a shell (north); Kaikias, also bearded, the bringer of hail (noth-east); Apeliotes, a young man bearing ears of corn and fruit (east); and Euros, wrapped in a cloak (south-east).

To the south of the tower is a building of the Roman period (1st c. AD) with the springing points of arches. Its original function is uncertain.

Adjoining the entrance to the excavated area is a marble **latrine** with seating for nearly 70.

On the north side of the market is a **mosque** built in the 15th c. in honour of Sultan Mehmet the Conqueror (Fetiye Camii); it is known to the Greeks as the Market Mosque (Djami tou Staropazaroú) and now used as an archaeological store.

To the east of the mosque is the doorway (inscriptions) of a Turkish medrese (Koranic school).

The Roman Agora with the Tower of the Winds

Salamís (Saronic island)

Area: 95 sq. km (37 sq. mi.)
Altitude: 0–365 m (0–4080 ft)
Population: 28,500
Chief town: Salamina (Kulúri)

Ferries (including car-ferries) from Pérama (5 km (3 mi.) west of Piraeus) and Megálo Péfko (Mégara).
Excursions from Piraeus.

Ferries

Salamis (modern Greek Salamina), is the largest island in the Saronic Gulf, with a richly articulated coastline. Its northern coast shuts off the Bay of Eleusis, which can be entered only through two narrow channels. Its largely karst hills and chalk ridges are covered in sparse woodland; the population, mainly composed of Albanian immigrants, is no longer able to subsist on the modest agriculture and tourist trade, so people have turned to the industries – mainly refineries and dockyards – that have been set up around the naval base in the north-east of the island and in the east of the Bay of Eleusis.

History The island was given its name (probably from "schalâm", meaning peace) by Phoenician settlers from Cyprus. It was conquered for Athens in 598 BC by Solon and Peisistratos. The old capital lay on a promontory between the bays of Kameteró and Ambeláki on the east coast, but in the 6th c. BC was moved further south-west near Ambeláki. Remains of its acropolis and the harbour can be seen below the water.

Salamis went into the history books when, in September of the year 480 BC, the battle-weakened Athenians under Themistocles convincingly

defeated the superior Persian fleet and nullified the plans of the Persian King Xerxes to extend his power westwards. The battle, taken by Aeschylus as the theme for his topical tragedy "The Persians", was fought in the waters east of Salamis between the islands of Ayios Georgios in the north and Psyttaleia and the Kynosura peninsula in the south.

Xerxes is said to have watched from a throne set up on Mount Aegaleos on the mainland.

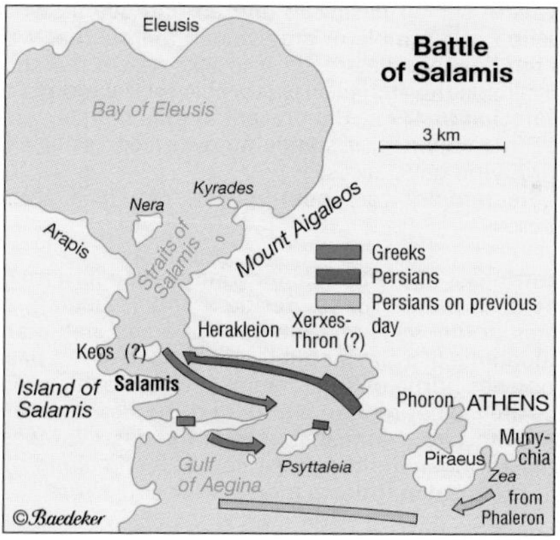

Sights

The capital of the island is Salamina (pop. 20,000), also known as Kulúri, lies in the north of the bay of the same name. Note the local archaeological museum.

Salamina

3 km (2 mi.) to the east is the main port of **Palúkia**.

Phaneroméni
monastery

This monastery lies on an attractive road some 6 km (4 mi.) west of Salamína. It is revered for its alleged appearances of the Virgin Mary, and has some fine frescoes. It was founded in 1661 on the site of an old sanctuary, material from which was used in its construction. A short way to the south are the remains of the little fort of Boudorón, dating from the 6th c. BC.

Schliemann's House   M 7

Location
Panepistimíu

Buses
023, 025, 230

Trolleybuses
6, 7, 12, 15

This palatial mansion was built by Ernst Ziller in 1878–9 for Heinrich Schliemann, the discoverer of Troy and of Mycenaean culture, and his Greek wife Sophia. Its name, Ilíou Mélathron ("Palace of Ilion"), commemorated the excavation of Troy. Along the front of the building is a two-storey loggia with columns of Pentelic marble, with paintings in the vaulting. There are also wall paintings in the interior. Schliemann is buried in the Cemetery of Athens (see entry).

In the little garden to the left is a copy of Phidias' "Wounded Amazon".

Soúnion

Location
70 km (43 mi.) on
the SE tip of Attica

Bus (orange)
To Soúnion from
Mavromateon
Ares Park

Open daily
10am–sunset

Admission fee

Every visitor to Athens should visit Cape Soúnion, not only for its magnificent sunsets but also for its famous temple of Poseidon, splendidly situated on the edge of a precipitous crag. Homer refers in the "Odyssey" (III, 278) to the "sacred cape" of Soúnion.

History In the 7th c. BC there was probably a simple altar here; about 600 BC the large kouroi figures now in the National Archaeological Museum (see entry) in Athens were set up beside it; and around 500 BC work began on the construction of a temple in grey-veined marble that was still unfinished when the Persians destroyed it in 480 BC. On the substructure of this earlier temple the architect responsible for the temple of Hephaistos in Athens erected in 449 BC the present marble temple, with exceptionally slender Doric columns. It stands on a terrace, artificially enlarged, to which a propylon gave access.

In the bay below the temple were **boat-houses**, of which some remains can still be seen.

On a flat-topped hill north-east of the temple (beyond the modern road) is a **sanctuary of Athena** of the 6th c. BC. Beside a small building, of which the lower courses of the walls and the base of a cult statue are preserved, are the foundations of a similar but larger temple, with a base of a cult statue. The roof was borne on four columns, in the fashion of a Mycenaean megaron. After suffering damage during the Persian wars the temple was rebuilt with two colonnades, not at the east and west ends as was the normal arrangement but at the east end and along the south side. The reason for this departure is a matter for conjecture.

Stadion   M 8

Location
Leofóros Ardíttou

Trolleybuses
2, 4, 11 (Stadion)

The Stadion, also known as the **Panathenaic Stadion**, lies between two low hills north-east of the Olympieion and south-east of the National Garden (see entries). The present Stadion, built of marble, is the largest building in Athens, with seating for 60,000 spectators. Although entirely modern it has the same form and occupies the same site as its ancient predecessor, in which the Panathenaic games were held.

History The ancient Stadion was built about 335 BC by the conservative politician Lykourgos, who also rebuilt the Lykeion and the Theatre of Dionysos (see entry). 500 years later (AD 140–144) it was provided with new marble seating by Herodes Atticus. The track was 204 m (669 ft) long by 33.46 m (110 ft) wide. Four double herms from the ends of the track were recovered by excavation. The races were run over a distance of a stade or stadion (185 m – 607 ft); in Athens in the two-stade race the runners turned at these herms.

Herodes Atticus, who was born in Marathon in AD 101 and died there in 177, was one of the great Maecenases of antiquity who rose to high dignities under Hadrian and Antoninus Pius. He was famous for his munificence, financing the Stadion and the Odeion (see entry) that bears his name in Athens, the renovation of the Stadion at Delphi, the provision of a water supply and the building of a nyphaeum at Olympia and the renovation of the spring of Peirene at Corinth.

In AD 133 Herodes Atticus erected on the hill of Ardettos, south-west of the Stadion, a temple of Tyche, in which the members of the Heliaia (lawcourt) swore their annual oath. He also had his tomb built on the hill on the north-east side of the Stadion; and the remains of a long structure found on the hill have been identified with this monument.

Although the Stadion was completely ruined and covered with earth and rubble its situation was known even before the excavation carried out by Ernst Ziller in 1869. Under the town plan drawn up by Schaubert and Kleanthes in 1832 Stadiou Street was intended to run straight from Omónia Square (see entry) to the Stadion instead of turning right into Sýntagma Square (see entry) as it does today. The plan was changed but the street name remained as it was.

When the Stadion was rebuilt for the first Olympic Games of modern times (1896) it was financed, as in the days of Herodes Atticus, by a wealthy private citizen. Yeoryios Averoff, who thus – like other modern Greeks, particularly those who have made their money abroad – continued the ancient tradition of the euergetes ("benefactor"). The **modern Stadion**, like the ancient one, has 47 tiers of seating and a rounded south-east end, the sphendone.

Sýntagma Square   M 7

Sýntagma Square (**Platía Syntágmatos**, Constitution Square), named after the constitution granted by King Otto on 3 September 1843, is the largest and most imposing square in Athens, the hub of the city's traffic and the starting-point of numerous bus services. In spite of this activity, however, the cafés in the centre of the square offer the opportunity for relaxation and refreshment. Around the square are numerous hotels and airline offices.

The parliament is situated in the square (see entry).

Location
City centre

Trolleybuses
1, 2, 4, 5, 9, 10,
11. 12, 15, 18

Buses 025, 040,
230 (Sýntagma)

Theatre of Dionysos   L 8

The Theatre of Dionysos is the oldest of the three architectural complexes on the southern slopes of the Acropolis – the others being the Odeion of Herodes Atticus (see entry) and the Stoa of Eumenes (see page 116).

History In the 6th c. BC Peisistratos transferred the cult of Dionysos from Eleutherai in the Kithairon hills (on the old road to Thebes) to Athens, where accordingly the god was known as Dionysos Eleuthereus, and a temple was built to house the old cult image from Eleutherai. In association with the cult of Dionysos – the god of drunkenness, of transformation, of ecstasy and the mask – the Theatre of Dionysos was built in a natural hollow on the slopes of the Acropolis. Nine building phases have been distinguished by Travlos, the first two dating from the 6th and 5th c.

Location
Dionysíou
Areopagítou
Street

Bus (blue and
white)
230 (Dionysíu
Areopagítou)

Open Tue.–Sun.
8.30am–3pm
Admission fee

The theatre and the temple precinct were separated about 420 BC, when a pillared hall facing south was built, involving the removal of the old temple, built of limestone. The brown breccia foundations of this later temple can be seen to the south of the remains of the hall.

About 330 BC the theatre's present stone tiers of seating were built. The 64 tiers (of which 25 survive in part), which could accommodate some 17,000 spectators, are divided into three sections by transverse gangways, and the lowest section is divided vertically into 13 wedges separated by stairways. In the front row are seats of honour inscribed with the names of the occupants; in the centre is the seat reserved for the priest of Dionysos Eleuthereus, decorated with reliefs and with post-holes in the ground pointing to the existence of a canopy. Behind the priest's seat, on a higher level, is a throne for the Emperor Hadrian (AD 117–138).

The tiers of seating rise up to a point directly below the Acropolis rock, where the cuttings for the top rows can be seen. In the rock face is a cave, once sacred to Dionysos, which was given an architectural façade by Thrasyllos in 320–319 BC; it has a tripod above it symbolising his victory as choregos. The two columns above the cave are tripod bases dating from the Roman period. The cave is now occupied by a small chapel of the Panayía Spiliótissa (Mother of God of the Cave).

The orchestra is paved with marble slabs and is surrounded by a marble barrier to provide protection from the wild beasts which took part in shows in Roman times. The stage buildings to the south, like the rest of the theatre, were much rebuilt in later periods. Here there are striking reliefs of Dionysiac scenes, dating from the Roman period; according to the most recent theory they were re-used in an orators' platform of the 5th c. AD.

The **importance** of the Theatre of Dionysos – of which there is a good general view from the south wall of the Acropolis – lies in the fact that it was built when tragedy was first being introduced, and indeed created, in Athens. This first drama was performed in 534 BC, probably in the Agora (see entry), by Thespis, a native of Ikaria (now Dionysius – see entry), who travelled about in a wagon with his company. This early dramatic form, in which a single actor performed with a chorus, was the beginning of a development which led in the 5th c. – the period of pride and confidence after the Persian wars – to the brilliant flowering of Greek tragedy. The works of the three great Attic tragedians were first performed in the Theatre of Dionysos in celebration of the Dionysiac cult; and here Aeschylus – who had fought at Marathon as a hoplite and was proud to have this recorded on his tombstone – as well as Sophocles and Euripides appeared in person. Thus the Theatre of Dionysos became the birthplace and origin of the European theatre.

To the east of the theatre stood the square **Odeion** built by Pericles, where excavations are in progress. Famed as the finest concert hall in Greece, this was completed in 443 BC and rebuilt between 65 and 52 BC after its destruction by Sulla in 86 BC.

Between the Odeion of Herodes Atticus (see entry) and the Theatre of Dionysos is the **Stoa of Eumenes**, built by King Eumenes II of Pergamon (197–160 BC), who not only erected magnificent buildings in his own city (Great Altar of Pergamon) but also sought to do honour to Athens by the building of this stoa. His example was followed by his brother and successor Attalos II (160–139 BC), who built the Stoa of Attalos in the Agora (see entry), probably using the same architect.

The Stoa of Eumenes differed from the Stoa of Attalos, which it exceeded in size, in having no rooms behind the double-aisled hall. It was thus not designed for the purposes of business but was merely a spacious promenade for visitors to the temple and theatre of Dionysos. It was two-storeyed, with Doric columns on the exterior, Ionic columns in the interior on the ground floor and capitals of Pergamene type on the upper floor. Since the stoa was built against the slope of the hill, it was protected by a retaining wall supported by piers and round arches; the arcades, originally faced with marble, can still be seen.

In 1060, during the Byzantine period, the buildings on the southern slopes of the Acropolis were incorporated in the fortifications of the citadel, the Rizokastron. The defensive wall, coming from the Propylaia, took in the outer walls of the Odeion of Herodes Atticus (see entry), the arcades of the Stoa of Eumenes and the walls of the parodoi of the Theatre of Dionysos.

In front of the east end of the Stoa of Eumenes are the foundations of the Monument of Nikias, erected in 320 BC to commemorate Nikias' victory as choregos. After its destruction by the Herulians in AD 267 material from this monument was built into the Beulé Gate of the Acropolis.

On a narrow terrace above the Stoa of Eumenes (see above), directly under the steep south face of the Acropolis (see entry), is the **Asklepieion**, the sanctuary of the healing god Asklepios, whose cult – initiated largely by Sophocles – was brought to Athens from Epidauros in 420 BC. The sanctuary is centred on two sacred springs.

The earliest part of the sanctuary lay at the **western end** of the precinct, where there are the foundations of a stoa and a small temple. A number of herms have been brought together in the stoa. At the west end of the complex is a rectangular system with polygonal walls dating from the same period. To the south is a later cistern.

The buildings in the **eastern part** of the precinct were erected about 350 BC. Immediately under the Acropolis rock, here hewn into a vertical face, is a stoa, originally two-storeyed, designed to accommodate the sick who came here to seek a cure. Associated with it is the cave containing a spring that is still credited with healing powers; and accordingly the cave is now used as a chapel.

Parallel to this stoa, which was rebuilt in Roman times, another stoa was constructed, also in Roman times, on the southern edge of this precinct; of this second stoa some remains survive.

Both stoas faced towards the centre of the precinct, in which stood the **temple**. This was oriented to the east and had four columns along the front (prostylos tetrastylos). The foundations of the temple and the altar which stood in front of it are still to be seen. In early Christian times a

The works of the great Tragedy writers Aeschylus, Sophocles and Euripides were performed in the Theatre of Dionysos

basilica was built over the remains of the temple and the altar, and some architectural fragments from this can be seen lying about the site.

On higher ground at the west end of the stoa is a **bothros**, a round pit for offerings, originally covered by a canopy borne on four columns. The bothros was an early form of the type of circular structure which reached its finest development in the Tholoi at Delphi and Epidauros.

Theatrical Museum   M 7

Location
Akademias 50
(basement of the
Culture Centre)

The Theatrical Museum (open Mon.–Fri. 9am–2.30pm) is hardly known to tourists. In charmingly arranged dressing-rooms can be found memorabilia of famous actors and actresses. Also of interest are photographs of the play "Antigone" when it was performed in Epidauros in 1905, for the first time in 2000 years, and of the same play performed in 1926 in the Herodion in Athens.

Directors' scripts going back to 1804, scenery, costumes, masks and a pretty collection of nostalgic theatre posters from all over Europe complete this most informative exhibition.

Themistoclean Walls

Until the Persian Wars only the Acropolis (see entry) was surrounded by walls; but after the destruction of Athens by the Persians in 480 BC Themistocles had a wall built round the city. The work was done in great haste, using the ruins of the monuments and buildings that had been destroyed.

A considerable stretch of these Themistoclean walls, with two gates (the Dipylon and the Sacred Gate), has been brought to light in the Kerameikos, another section north of the Olympeion (see entries). Further remains of the walls were found during the construction of the government buildings over the church of the Ayía Dýnamis (see entry) in Mitropóleos Street, at 6–8 Dragatsaniou Street (see Klafthmónos Square) and on the site of the Divani Zafolia Hotel, in Parthenónos Street, to the south of the Acropolis. These two latter sections are open to the public.

The city's defences were strengthened between 465 and 460 BC by the construction of the **Long Walls**, which ran south-west and south from Athens and were designed to secure communications between Athens and the ports of Piraeus (see entry) and Phaleron. The road to Piraeus was further protected by a parallel wall built by Pericles in 445 BC.

This defensive system was completed in 337 BC by the construction of the **Diateichisma**, an intermediate wall between the Hill of the Nymphs and the Hill of the Muses (see entries) that shortened the defensive line.

Thorikós

Excursion
79 km (49 mi.) SE
Bus (orange)
Mavromateon,
Ares Par

Trolleybuses
1, 2, 3, 4, 5, 7, 11,
12, 13

11 km (7 mi.) north of Cape Soúnion (see entry) and 2 km (1¼ mi.) north of Lávrion, near the coast (to the east of the road), is the site of ancient Thorikós, on a hill overlooking the bay of Lávrion, which was fortified in 490 BC to provide defence against Persian attack.

There was a settlement here in Mycenaean times, as is shown by two nearby tholos tombs (between the two summits of the hill and on its eastern slopes).

The most notable structure on the site is the theatre (5th–4th c. BC), which belonged to a sanctuary of Dionysos. It is of rather archaic type, with an orchestra which is neither circular nor semicircular, as was the usual style, but almost rectangular. In consequence the auditorium also departs from the usual circular form.

University   L/M 6/7

The classicist National Library

Location
Panepistimíou
(Venizélou) St
Buses
024, 230
(Panepistimíu)

Trolleybuses
6, 7, 12, 15

Buses
024, 230

The University, Academy and National Library in Panepistimíou (University) Street – now officially Venizélou Street – together with the New Palace (see entry), are the most striking achievements of the young kingdom of Greece in the field of architecture and town planning. The three buildings were designed by the Hansen brothers of Copenhagen.

The **University**, a plain neo-classical building with restrained ornament, was built in 1839–41 by Christian Hansen (1803–83). Behind the columns of the portico, above the doorway, is a representation of King Otto, who initiated the project, surrounded by Muses. In front of the entrance are figures of Kapodistrias, who as Govenor of Greece (1827–31) proclaimed the foundation of the university, the writer and scholar Adamantios Korais (1748–1833) and also W. M. Gladstone. Immediately in front of the façade are the statues of the poet Rigas Pherraios and Patriarch Gregory IV, who were murdered by the Turks in 1789 and 1821 respectively. Inside, the portico, stair-well and aula all display examples of the fine ornamentation of the period.

The two flanking buildings were designed by Christian Hansen's younger brother Theophil (1813–91) in a richer style. The design for both buildings was prepared in 1859, and work began in that year on the **Academy of Sciences** (to right of the University), which was financed by a Greek living in Vienna, Baron Sina. The building was not completed, however, until 1885.

When restored in 1982 the Ionic columned hall was returned to its original colouring. The carved pediments display the gods of Olympia. In front of the buildings are seated sculptures of Plato and Socrates, and to the side of them, on tall Ionic columns, are the deities Athena and Apollo.

The complex was completed when Theophil Hansen built the **National Library**, to the left of the University, in 1887–91. In 1903 the stock of the National Library was combined with that of the University Library.

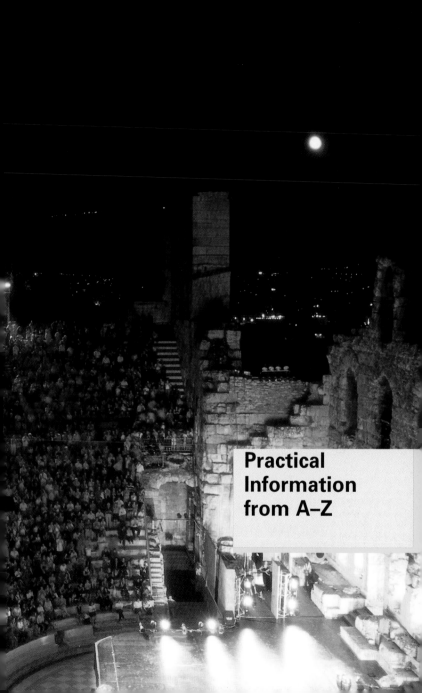

**Practical
Information
from A–Z**

Practical Information

Arriving

By air
: The majority of visitors to Athens travel by air. There are direct flights from London and the US. In addition there are numerous charter flights during the holiday season to Athens, usually carrying passengers who have booked one of the many package tours offered by travel operators.

By road
: It is a very long drive from any of the channel ports to Greece and in view of the situation in the former Yugoslavia motorists are still advised not to travel through that country. The alternative for those who insist on taking their own vehicle is to drive to one of the Italian ports from which car ferries operate to Piraeus (see Ferries).

By sea
: There are no direct services between Great Britain and Greece, and the only possible way of getting there by sea is to travel on one of the ferries operating from the Italian ports on the Adriatic. At present this is the only practicable alternative to flying. However, visitors with only limited time at their disposal should be aware that this means of getting to Greece is likely to take at least three days in either direction and will certainly not be cheap.

By rail
: There are services to Athens via Paris and thence by ferry from Brindisi, but the journey is long and fairly slow. Services via Germany (Cologne) through the former Yugoslavia are at present suspended and depend on the political situation in the latter country becoming stabilised. In any case the journey is long and tiring, taking three days from London to Athens, with further time necessary on a ferry to the island.

Air Travel

Airlines

Olympic Airways
: Head Office:
Leofórus Sýngrou 96; tel. (01) 9269111

Odos Othonos 6 (Sýntagma Square); tel. 9292555

Athens airport; tel. 9363363

Olympic Airways Domestic
: Olympic Airways have a comprehensive network of services connecting Athens with the following places: Áktion, Alexandrúpolis, Chaniá (Crete), Chios Corfu (Kérkyra), Iráklion (Crete), Ioánnina, Kalamáta, Kárpathos, Kásos, Kastellorízo, Kastoriá, Kaválla, Kefallinía, Kos Kozáni, Kýthira, Larisa, Lemnos, Léros, Melos, Mýkonos, Mytilíni (Lesbos), Páros, Rhodes, Sámos, Santoríni, Sitía, Skiáthos, Skýros, Thessaloníki, Zákynthos

British Airways
: Odos Othonos 10; tel. (01) 3250601

Airport

Athens's airport (aerodrómion) Hellenikon (Ellinikoú) is 12 km (7½ mi.) south-east of the city centre, close to the coast.

The Eastern Terminal is for international foreign airlines, while the Western Terminal serves domestic and international flights operated by Olympic Airways.

The new Charter Terminal is for charter flights only.

Eastern Terminal: Airport buses

Express bus 91 (Eastern Terminal–Sýntagma Square/Amalias–Eastern Terminal) operates daily 6am–midnight, every 20 minutes.

Express bus 19 (Eastern Terminal–Western Terminal–Piraeus port–Western Terminal–Eastern Terminal) operates daily 8am–8pm, hourly.

Western Terminal:

Express bus 19 and Olympic Airways airport bus (Western Terminal–Sýngrou–Sýntagma Square/corner of Amalias– Othonos–Western Terminal) operates daily 6am–8pm, every 30 minutes.

There are some (blue and white) municipal bus services that stop at both airport terminals. Large pieces of luggage are not permitted on these buses.

Beaches

It is now common knowledge that many stretches of the Mediterranean coastline are not as clean and unspoilt as was the case twenty or thirty years ago. This is particularly true of the Attic Riviera on the Saronic Gulf where the water quality has been heavily affected by the shipping and effluent from the Athens area. Bathing near the city is therefore inadvisable.

As well as the environmental pollution there are dangerous currents off the Attic coast, and occasionally large shoals of jellyfish make bathing hazardous. Sharks, stingray, sea urchins, poisonous dragon fish ("drakena") and other not exactly harmless sea creatures provide excitement from time to time.

Glyfada, close to the airport, is the most popular and well equipped beach. Others include Kavuri, Vula, Vuliagméni, Varkiza, Lagonissi (exclusive beach recreation centre) and Soúnion.

Attic Riviera (Apollo coast)

There are less crowded resorts at Vravrona (Brauron), Loútsa, Marathón, Nea Makri and Rhamnús.

North-east Attic coast

Several luxury hotels have been built near the beach at Kinetta, between Athens and Corinth.

Kinetta

Pretty, unspoilt coves and beaches can still be found on the islands of Aegina, Póros, Hýdra and Spétsae.

Islands

Boat Services

Information about the rental of boats and yachts can be obtained from:

Association of Brokers
Alkonis Street 36
Paleó Fáliro
Tel. 9816582.

Camping

Camping anywhere other than on recognised campsites is not permitted in Greece.

Classification of campsites

The majority of Greek campsites are supervised by the tourist authorities and fall into the following categories: A = excellent amenities, B = good, C = satisfactory.

Campsites around Athens

Akropolis (B)
15 km (9 mi.) outside the city near Nea Kifissia, on the main road to Lamia; tel. 8075253
Open Apr.–Oct.

Athens Camping (C)
Peristeri, Leophoros Athinon 198; tel. 5814101, 581414, fax 5820353
Open all year

Dionissiotis (A)
18 km (11 mi.) out of the city near Nea Kifissia, on the main road to Lamia; tel. 8071494
Open all year

Varkiza Beach (B)
25 km (16 mi.) south-east of the city centre near Varkiza; tel. 8973613
Open all year

Karabateas (A)
Near Dafni; tel. 5981150
Open all year

Nea Kifissia (C)
Near Nea Kifissia; tel. 8075579
Open Apr.–Oct.

Vakchos (C)
Súnion, Assimaki; tel. 029239263
Open Jul.–Sep.

Varkiza Beach (B)
Bei Várkiza; tel. 8973613
Open all year

Vula (A)
Vula, Alkyonidon 3; tel. 8952712/1641
Open all year

Information

Information about campsites can be obtained from ELPA (see Motoring), and the Greek Camping Association, Solonos 102, GR–10680, Athens; tel. 3621560, fax 3465262/5820353.

Car Rental

There are numerous car rental firms in Athens and Piraeus. An international driving licence is necessary. Chauffeur-driven limousines can also be hired. Tariffs vary according to the type of car, the duration of the hire and the time of year.

Car rental companies (selection)

Avis, Amalias 48; tel. 3224951/5, fax 3220216
Budget, Syngroú 8; tel. 9214771/3, fax. 9224444
Europcar/InterRent, Syngroú 4; tel. 9248810, fax. 9221440

Hertz, Syngroú 12; tel. 9220102/4

These companies also have branches at the airport.

Conversions

To convert metric to imperial multiply by the imperial factor; e.g. 100 km equals 62 mi. (100 x **0.62**).

1 metre	**3.28** feet, **1.09** yards	Linear measure
1 kilometre (1000 m)	**0.62** mile	
1 square metre	**1.2** square yards, **10.76** square feet	Square measure
1 hectare	**2.47** acres	
1 square kilometre (100 ha)	**0.39** square mile	
1 litre (1000 ml)	**1.76** pints (**2.11** US pints)	Capacity
1 kilogram (1000 grams)	**2.21** pounds	
1 metric ton (1000 kg)	**0.98** ton	

°C	°F	°C	°F	
−5	23	20	68	Temperature
0	32	25	77	
5	41	30	86	
10	50	35	95	
15	59	40	104	

Currency

The Greek unit of currency is the drachma. There are banknotes for 50, 100, 200, 500, 1000 and 5000 dr. and coins in denominations of 5, 10, 20 and 50 dr.

The branches of some of the larger Greek banks are open 24 hours a day at the Eastern and Western terminals of Athens Ellinikó airport.
    Foreign currency can be exchanged at the reception desks of some hotels, but the rates are generally lower than elsewhere. Some post offices in Athens have exchange kiosks.
    Exchange rates can be obtained from banks, exchange and tourist offices, and are published in the principal national newspapers.

Exchange

There are no restrictions on the import of foreign currency either in the form of travellers' cheques or cash. Foreign currency up to 1000 US dollars per person may be taken out again within a year; larger amounts may be taken out if they have been declared in writing on entry. Visitors may take into Greece 100,000 drachma in Greek currency and 20,000 dr. may be taken out (in banknotes of up to 1000 dr.). Greek money can only be changed back on production of a flight ticket at a special counter inside the Eastern terminal of the international airport.

Import and export

See Opening Hours

Banks

The major credit cards are accepted in larger hotels and many shops.

Credit cards

It is advisable to take Eurocheques or travellers' cheques. Eurocheques are accepted in many shops up to a limit of 30,000 dr.

Travellers' cheques

Customs Regulations

Import — Visitors to Greece can import without payment of duty personal items as well as new articles for their own use or for gifts up to a value of 137,000 drachmas providing no single item is worth more than 77,500 drachmas. They may also take in duty free 300 cigarettes (or 75 cigars, or 150 cigarillos, or 400 grams of tobacco), 5 boxes of matches, 2 packs of cards, 4 litres of alcoholic drink, 1.5 litres of spirits, up to 10 kg of sweets and cakes, 75 grams perfume and 0.375 litre eau de cologne.

Items for personal use comprise the following: one camera with a reasonable number of films, one film camera with projector, one pair of binoculars, one portable radio, one portable record player and 10 records, one tape recorder, one portable typewriter, sport and camping equipment, one bicycle, one gas-pistol, sports articles (skis, windsurfing equipment, etc.), one or two sporting guns and up to 20 cartridges per person. All these articles must be entered on the owner's passport.

The import of flowers, plants and radio transmitters is prohibited.

CB radios installed in cars may be brought into Greece but not used.

Export — Visitors may take out provisions for the journey up to a value of 50 US dollars and souvenirs up to a value of 150 US dollars. The export of antiquities and works of art is prohibited. There are no restrictions concerning the export of copies.

Souvenirs from Greece up to a value of about ú300, as well as 1 kg coffee, 200 grams tea, 5 litres of wine and 300 cigarettes (or 150 cigarillos, or 75 cigars or 400 grams tobacco) may be taken into an EU country.

Electricity

220 V AC; on ships frequently 110 V. Appliances have standard European plugs; British plugs require an adapter.

Embassies and Consulates

United Kingdom — 1 Ploutárchou Street
Tel. 7236211/9

United States — Leofóros Vas. Sofías 91
Tel. 7212951, 7218401

Canada — 4 Ioannou Gennadioú Street
Tel. 7254011/9

Australia — 37, D. Soutsou St.
Tel. 6447303

Emergencies

The most useful source of assistance for the tourist is the Tourist Police; tel. 171.

Tel. 100	Police
Tel. 106. Weekend and holiday duty service: tel. 105 (surgery hours usually 6–9pm)	Hospital casualty
Tel. 166	First Aid
Tel. 150	Red Cross
Tel. 199	Fire brigade
Athens: tel. 52301115 Piraeus: 4113832	Traffic police
Tel. 108	Coastguard
Tel. 104	ELPA (roadside assistance)

Lost Property Office (grafío evréseos apolesténdon)

Aliens Service, Central Lost Property Office, Alexandras 173 (10th floor) Tel. 770–57 11	Central office
Traffic police lost property office, Agiu Konstantinou 38 Tel. 523–0111	Taxis, buses

Entertainment

Theatre and concert programmes are obtainable from the Athens Festival Office, Stádiou 4 (Spyromiliou Arcade); tel. 3221459, 3223111/9.
   Programmes are also published in the daily newspaper "This Week in Athens".

The Athens festival takes place from June to October. Main performances are held in the Herodes Atticus theatre (slopes of the Acropolis). Advance ticket sales from the Amerikis Stoá.

Athens festival

National Theatre, Konstantinou 20; tel. 5233322
Olympia Theatre, Akademias 59–61; tel. 3612461
Athens College Theatre, Psychiko; tel. 6717523
Deree Pierce Theatre, Paraskevi, Gravias 6; tel. 6593250
Herodes Atticus Odeion
Roman Agorá
Eleftherias Park Theatre
Petra Theatre, Petrupolis
Tenta Theatre, Sýngrou 103
Argyrupolis Theatre
Glyfáda Theatre
Veakaio Theatre, Piraeus
Delfinario, Faliron

Theatres
(including music
halls)

Dora Stratou; performances May–Sep. in the Philopappos Theatre; tel. 3 244395, 921–4650
Aliki Theatre, Amerikis 4; tel. 9214659
   Performances of folk theatre also in the tavernas in the Pláka.

Folklore

Spirópulo Theatre, Galátsi, Ersis 9

Shadow theatre

Mégaro Musikís Athinón, Vass. Sofías/Kokkáli; tel. 7282333
Parnassos Hall, Georgiou Karytsi 8; tel. 3238745

Concert halls

A folk dancing group performing in the Philopappos Theatre

	Gloria Theatre, Ippokratus 7; tel. 3626702
Pop and rock concerts	Lykabettós Open Air Theatre; tel. 7227209, 7227233
Son et lumière	From April 1st until October 31st a *son et lumière* show is presented every evening (9pm daily in English) with illumination of the Acropolis and commentaries bringing out the highlights of the Greek Classical period. The best views are obtained from the neighbouring Pnyx hill. For information tel. 3221459 or 3223111. Tickets from offices of the Athens Festival Office, Stádiou 4 (Spyromiliou Arcade) and at the entrance (Pnyx).

Events

January 1st	St Vassilios (St Basil's Day); Kalanda singing on the streets, cutting of the "Vassilo Pitta" (a New Year cake often containing coins).
January 6th	Trion Ierarchon (Three Kings' Day); water festival in Piraeus, beginning of the carnival period with costume balls, festivals.
February	Carnival Sunday: procession through Athens centre (Omónia Square–Zappion). Katharí Deftéra ("Cleaner Monday"): kite flying on the hills, preparation for Lent with unleavened bread, fish, seafood, salads and wine.
March 25th (National Day)	Military parade

Candlelit procession	Good Friday (movable date)
Easter is the most important festival in Greece. Mass is celebrated at midnight on Easter Saturday, reaching its climax with the cry "Christós Anésti" (Christ is risen). It is marked by cannon fire, fireworks, egg-kicking, and presents are exchanged. The traditional meal is roast lamb. Tsureki is the typical Easter cake decorated with a hard-boiled egg, dyed red.	Easter (movable date)
Labour Day processions and Feast of Flowers.	May 1st
Son et lumière show every evening at the Acropolis. (See Theatres)	April–October
Acropolis rally	Late May
Maritime festival at Piraeus	June/July
Athens Festival, See Theatres Epidaurus Festival, See Theatres	June–September
Wine festival in Dafni	July/September
Assumption; festival of Mother of God	August 15th
Maritime festival on Spétsae. International Tourism Day	September
National Day; military parades	October 28th

Excursions

Day trips to Delphi, Epidauros, Corinth, Mycenae and Cape Soúnion can be booked at travel agents, especially around Sýntagma Square, and at many hotel receptions. There is usually a choice of booking an excursion with lunch included or excluded – it is advisable, however, not to take the inclusive option but to visit a taverna of your own choice for lunch. It is also possible to reach the places listed below by public transport.

Excursions by coach

An excursion to the ancient site of worship for Apollo in Delphi is one of the highpoints of a holiday in Greece. Delphi, famous for its oracles, is situated in splendid isolation on the south-western slopes of Mount Parnassus. Remains dating back from the 6th to the 2nd centuries BC have been excavated here, and are exhibited in the Delphi Museum.

★★Delphi
Location: 165 km (103 mi.) NW

Another important ancient sanctuary is Eleusis where the cult of mysteries was celebrated which harks back to the goddess Demeter. Finds dating from Mycaenian to Classical times are exhibited in the Eleusis Museum.

★Eleusis
Location: 22 km (14 mi.) W

In Epidauros, situated on the Argolis peninsula in the Peloponnese, was the temple of Asklepios (Aesculapius), the god of healing. His symbol – the snake coiled around the rod of Asklepius – is still used as an emblem in the medical profession, to signify doctors, pharmacists, etc.
    The ancient **theatre** is the best preserved complex of its kind and famous for its unique acoustics.

★★Epidauros
Location: 112 km (70 mi.) SW

Corinth is situated on the isthmus, measuring only 6 km (3.7 mi.) across, between the Greek mainland and the Peloponnese peninsula, which is cut through by the **Corinth Canal** (cut up to 80 m (262 ft) deep into surrounding rocks but only 24.5 m (80 ft) wide), built between 1882 and 1893 by a French company. In **Ancient Corinth**, the interesting remains

★★Corinth
Location: 60 km (37 mi.) W

of the old town can be seen, and the fortifications on the **Acrocorinth** outcrop (574 m (1883 ft) high) date back to Antiquity.

★ Marathón
Location: 42 km
(26 mi.) NE

The village of Marathón, situated on the eastern Attic coast, is famous for the first great battles between the Greeks and the Persians (490 BC) in which the Athenians were victorious despite the fact that the Persian troops were far superior in numbers. There are two burial mounds containing the ashes of the war dead on the battlefield of Marathón, 4 km (2.5 mi.) south-east of the village.

★ Mycenae
Location: 105 km
(65 mi.) SW

Once you have seen the unique finds of Mycenae in the National Archaeological Museum in Athens, it is worth visiting the site, too. It was excavated in 1876 by Heinrich Schliemann, following the reports of ancient writers. The famous gold masks and jewellery were discovered in the **royal tombs**. Equally well known is the **Lion Gate**.

Soúnion

See entry

Excursions by ship

Ships and hydrofoils depart from the harbours of Páleo Fàliro, Zéa and Piraeus for Hýdra, Póros, Spétsai and Aegina. All the islands can easily be reached on a day trip.

Cruises

Piraeus is important both as a port of departure and as a port of call in the Mediterranean. From Piraeus there are day excursions to the islands in the Saronic Gulf as well as longer cruises in the Aegean, to Asia Minor, Crete and destinations in Israel, Egypt and the Black Sea.
   The price of day cruises usually include transfers from the hotel as well as a lunchtime buffet. Overnight cruises are all inclusive (reductions for children are available).

Sightseeing

There are numerous half- or all-day sightseeing tours available, where English is spoken. The "Athens by Night" bus tours are especially popular, and usually include a short stay at the Pnyx where the sound and light show on the Acropolis can be experienced. However, the folklore evenings, offering food in the Pláka and folklore performances, are perhaps not to be recommended, because neither hold any authenticity.

Guided tours

There are paid guides available to help you discover Athens. Find out about their quality at the Tourist Information offices and make sure you come to an agreement about the fee before you set off.

Ferries

There are regular ferries from Venice, Ancona and Brindisi to Athens (Piraeus). The ferries from Ancona, Bari and Brindisi usually also call at Corfu and Igoumenitsa.
   Drivers of camping vehicles or of vehicles towing caravans should enquire from the company or travel agent in advance about the permitted maximum lengths of vehicles on individual ferries. See also Arriving.

Car ferries during high season

ITALY–GREECE	FREQUENCY	OPERATOR
Ancona–Igoumenitsa–Corfu–Pátras	2/3 times weekly	Strintzis Lines
Ancona–Igoumenitsa–Pátras	5 times weekly 6 times weekly	Anek Lines Minoan Lines
Ancona–Pátras	daily	Superfast Ferries
Bari–Pátras	daily daily	Superfast Ferries Ventouris Ferries

Bari–Igoumenitsa	4 times weekly	Marlines
Bari–Corfu–Igoumenitsa–Keffallonia–Pátras	3 times weekly	Ventouris Ferries
Brindisi–Corfu–Igoumenitsa–Pátras	daily	Adriarica
Brindisi–Corfu–Igoumenitsa	almost daily 5 times weekly	Fragline Ferries Strintzis Lines
Brindisi–Igoumenitsa	3/4 times weekly	Hellenic. Med. Lines
Brindisi–Pátras	3/4 times weekly	Hellenic. Med. Lines
Triest–Corfu–Igoumenitsa–Pátras	4 times weekly	Anek Lines
Venice–Igoumenitsa–Corfu–Pátras	3/4 times weekly daily (Apr.–Oct.)	Minoan Lines
	2–3 times daily	Strintzis Lines

Food and Drink

Mealtimes

Greek breakfast is usually a simple affair – a cup of coffee or glass of milk accompanied by a few slices of bread with butter or margarine and jam (usually apricot or strawberry). Luxury hotels provide substantial buffet-style breakfasts.

Breakfast

The Greeks just have a small meal or snack at lunchtime with many restaurants only offering a limited choice of menus. There is a greater selection in tourist areas.

Lunch

The main meal is served in the evening from about 9pm.

Dinner

Food

Greek hotels provide a mainly international cuisine, with some Greek dishes and garnishings added for a touch of colour. In restaurants (see entry) the national cuisine predominates, showing Eastern (mainly Turkish) influences and making much use of olive oil, garlic and herbs.

The Greek table will always be supplied with bread psomi, salt alati, pepper piper and sugar zakhari.

There is a wide choice of hors d'œuvres. In addition to the appetisers (mezes) served with the aperitif, the range includes prawns, seafood, vine-leaves stuffed with rice (dolmádes) and salads (salátes).

Hors d'œuvres(orektik)

Greek soups are very substantial and are often made with eggs and lemon juice. Fasolada is a popular thick bean soup; others include pepper soup (pipéri soúpa), made with vegetables and meat, clear bouillon (somós creátos) and some excellent fish soups (psárosoupes). Both meat and fish dishes are often flavoured with lemon juice.

Soups

The favourite meats in Greece are lamb (arnáki) and mutton (arní), usually served roasted or grilled. Also very popular are souvlaki (meat grilled on the spit) and yiros (meat grilled on a vertical spit and cut off in thin slices). Kokorétsi are lamb entrails roasted on the spit. Grilled chicken is becoming increasingly popular.

Meat (kréas)

These are popular and include patitío, a dish of pasta and minced meat, and moussáka, made with aubergines and minced meat. These dishes are usually baked.

Composite dishes

131

Food and Drink

Vegetables

Typical Mediterranean vegetables are artichokes (angináres), aubergines (melitsánes), courgettes (kolokithákia) and peppers (piperié), usually stuffed or cooked in oil. Horta, boiled spinach, flavoured with lemon juice, is popular.

Salads

Salads include lettuce (marulli), tomato salad (tomáto saláta), asparagus salad (sparánga saláta) and Greek or "country" salad (khoriatikí), made of lettuce, tomatoes, olives and ewe's cheese (feta).

Fish (psári)

Fish and seafood feature prominently on the Greek menu. The commonest species are sea bream (sinagrída, tsipoúra), sole (gl¢ssa), red mullet (barboúni) and tunny (t¢nnos), together with lobster (astak¢s), mussels (mydia), squid (kalamári) and octopus (oktap¢di). In many restaurants the customer can choose the fish and have it cooked to his own taste.

Desserts (desér)

The commonest desserts are an ice (pagotó) or fruit, of which there is a wide choice, varying according to season – watermelons (karpoúsi), musk-melons (pepóni), peaches (rodákina), pears (akhládia), apples (mila), oranges (portokália), grapes (stafylia) and figs (syka).

Cheese (tyrí)

Most Greek cheeses are made from ewe's or goat's milk, which is also used to produce yoghurt (yaoúrti).

Drinks

Wine (krasí)

The commonest Greek drink is wine, either red (mávro krasí) or white (áspro krasí); there are both dry and sweet wines. The everyday table wines are resinated to improve their keeping qualities (krasí retsináto), giving them a characteristic sharp taste that takes time to appreciate; they are, however, good for the digestion and stimulating to the appetite.

The ancient Greeks also had a preference for resinated wine, and traces of resin (retsína) have been found in the oldest amphoras. The resin is added during fermentation. There are also unresinated red and white wines that comply with EU directives; they are identified by the letters VQPRD on the label. The Greek wines best known outside Greece are the white wine of Sámos and Mavrodaphne, a sweet red wine.

Beer (bíra)

The brewing of beer in Greece dates from the reign of King Otto I, a native of Bavaria. The beers, almost all brewed to Bavarian recipes, are usually excellent. The consumption of beer in Greece has increased considerably in recent years.

Spirits (pnevmatódi potá)

The commonest aperitif is (ouzo), an aniseed-flavoured spirit usually drunk with the addition of water, which gives it a milky colouring. Rakí is similar but stronger. Mástikha is a liqueur made from the bark of the mastic tree (pistacia lentiscus). Greek brandy (knoyák) is fruity and relatively light.

Soft drinks

These include mineral water (metallikó neró, sóda), the very popular orangeade and lemonade (portokaláda, lemonáda) and freshly pressed fruit juices (portokaláda fréska).

Coffee (kafés, kafedáki)

Coffee comes in different strengths and degrees of sweetness – e.g. kafés glykis vrastos (with plenty of sugar), kafés varis glykos (strong and sweet), kafés elafros (light), the popular kafés metrios (medium strength with little sugar), and kafés sketos (without any sugar).

Frappé

Frappé is a coffee-flavoured cold drink made from powder.

Tea (tsai)

In addition to "black" tea (mávro tsai) there are various herbal teas, including peppermint tea (tsai ménda) and tsai touvounnoú, an infusion of mountain herbs.

Kafenion

The coffee house (kafenion) plays an important part in the life of the Greeks and is frequented mainly by men. It is not merely a place for drinking coffee, but has in a sense taken over the function of the ancient Greek agora as a place for meeting friends, conversation, playing games and doing business.

There are also patisseries (zacharoplasteion) where the women go. Cakes, pastries and ice cream are served with French coffee and other beverages. Greek pastries tend to be very sweet.

Patisseries

Health

KAT, Kifissia, Nikis 2; tel. 801–4411/20
Voula Hospital, Askepion, Vass. Pavlu 1; tel. 895–8301/05

Casualty hospitals
(nosokomio)

Pediatric Centre, Marussi, Distomu/Kifissias 5; tel. 682–0140

Children's
hospital

The Greek Red Cross (3rd Septemvriu 21) provides emergency first aid free of charge.

Under European Union regulations British visitors to Greece are entitled to medical care under the Greek social insurance scheme on the same basis as Greek citizens. Before leaving home they should apply to their local Social Security office for form E 111 and the accompanying leaflet on "How to get medical treatment in other European Union countries".
    These arrangements may not cover the full cost of medical treatment, and it is advisable, therefore, even for EU citizens, to take out short-term health insurance. Visitors from non-EU countries should certainly do so.

Medical Insurance

Chemists

There are numerous chemist shops in Athens. They can be identified by a cross on a round plate above the entrance and the word ΦΑΡΜΑΚΕΙΟ (FARMAKIO).
    Every chemist shop displays a notice giving the address of the nearest chemist on the emergency roster.
    The "Athens News" also lists, under the heading "Chemists – Pharmacies", chemists open at night and on Sundays and public holidays. In emergency dial 107.

See entry

Opening hours

Hotels

Athens and the immediate surrounding area are well provided with hotels. Advance reservation is, however, advisable, particularly during the main holiday season at Easter, Whitsun and from June to September.
Information and reservations:
Xenodochiako Epimiletirio
Odós Stadíu 24, GR-10564 Athens
Tel. 3310022/6, fax 3236862, 3225449.

Reservations

Karageorgi 2, building of the Greek National bank.
Tel. 3237193.

Information
centre

Open Mon.–Thurs. 8.30 am – 2 pm, Fri. 8.30 am – 1.30 pm, Sat. 9 am –
12.30 pm.

Price   Prices vary according to season and often 16 per cent tax is added.
Standards of comfort may not be the same as in Britain or America.

Categories   Greek hotels (xenodochio) are officially classified in six categories (L=
luxury, A, B, C, D and E) and most visitors will look for accommodation
in one of the first four categories. The following list is arranged according to these categories.
   b. = beds; SP = swimming pool; T = tennis. The most outstanding
hotels have been noted with a Baedeker star.

Hotels in Central Athens

Category L   ★Athens Hilton, Leofóros Vass. Sofias 46, tel. 7250201, fax 7253110, 862
b., SP.
Oldest of the numerous modern luxury hotels in town. Favoured meeting point of the high society. Four restaurants, three bars, fitness studio,
bank and shops.

★Grande Bretagne, Sýntagma, tel. 3314444, fax 3330000, 668 b.
The most richly traditional of all the Athens luxury hotels is located
directly opposite the parliament building, on the busy Sýntagma
Square. State guests stay in this hotel: the presidential suite is the most
expensive suite in Athens at 300 000 Drs. per night. Nobility, VIPs and
politicians all meet here. The building was constructed in 1862 for the
king's guests. It has been used as a hotel since 1872 and is bursting with
antiques. The lobby is all marble, the ball room is fin-de-siècle and there
is a winter garden. The rooms, all with marble baths, offer an exquisite
view of the Acropolis.

★Saint George Lycabettós, Kolonáki, Kleomenus 2, tel. 7290711–19, fax
7290439, 278 b., SP.
This luxury hotel has the most atmosphere and personal attention of all
luxury hotels in Athens. Located on the Lycabettós hill in the distinguished area of Kolonáki. Very close to the centre, yet very quiet. Many
rooms and the swimming pool offer a magnificent town view. Amongst
the regulars are numerous artists and authors.

Category A   Andromeda, Timoléontos Vassu 22, tel. 6437302, fax 6466361, 52 b., SP.
Small luxury hotel, opened in 1991, near the Lycabettós hill. Postmodern
interior, favoured by Greek business people. Choice of Italian and
Polynesian dishes

★Electra Palace, Nicudimu 18, tel. 3241401–7, fax 3241875, 180 b., SP.
Modern, quiet hotel – the best in the Pláka. Swimming pool on the roof
terrace with marvellous view of the Acropolis. The bustling Pláka is right
on your doorstep.

Esperia Palace, Stadíu 22, tel. 3238001, fax 3238100, 338 b.
On the busy Stadíu street. Most rooms with balcony or terrace. Very
pleasant bar and dining room. The Athineos Restaurant serves good
Greek and international food.

★King Minos, Piraeus 1, tel. 5231111–18, fax 5231361, 287 b., SP.
Modern hotel on the busy Omónia Square, renovated in 1987, soudproof
windows. Roof terrace with swimming pool. Panoramic town view.
Restaurant with Greek and international dishes.

Novotel Athens, Michail Voda 4–6, tel. 8250422/30, fax 8837816, 361 b., SP.

Modern hotel from the well known chain. Outside the centre, near the main road to Pátras and therefore recommended for car travellers. Roof garden.

Olympic Palace, Filellínon 16, tel. 3237611, fax 3225583, 168 b.
Central location, near Sýntagma Square on the outskirts of the Pláka.

President, Kifissias 43, tel 6924600, fax 6924900, 912 b., SP.
Large modern hotel outside the centre , with roof garden and disco. Good bus connection into town.

Arethusa, Metropóleos 6–8, tel. 3229431, fax 3229439, 158 b. Category B
Central location, near Sýntagma Square. Large rooms, some with a terrace and a wonderful view. Restaurant on the roof terrace.

Athenian Inn, Charitos 22, tel. 7238097, fax 7242268.
Unusual, small hotel, with family atmosphere. On the foot of the Lykabettós. Open fireplace. Decorated with wall pantings by local artists.

Athens Gate, Syöngrú 10, tel. 9238302, fax 9238781, 199 b.
Modern hotel near the Olympieion, on the edge of the Pláka. Cafeteria and roof terrace with view of the Acropolis.

⋆Omiros, Apóllonos 15, tel. 3235486, 80 b.
Small medium class hotel, in a quiet location yet in the middle of the Pláka, in a road with hotels. Efficient interior, roof terrace with view of the Acropolis.

Oscar, Sámu 25, tel. 8834215/9, fax 8216368, 207 b., SP.
Located near the main train station Laríssis. Roof terrace with swimming pool. Good bus connection to the Omónia and Sýntagma Squares.

⋆Stanley, Odysseos 1, tel. 5240142/5, fax 5244611, 714 b., SP.
Located between the Omónia Square and the main train station Laríssis. Roof terrace with swimming pool.

Acropolis View, Wébster 10, tel. 9217303/5, fax 9230705, 47 b. Category C
Small hotel in a relatively quiet street next to the Acropolis, around a 15 minutes' walk away from the Pláka.

Aphrodite, Apóllonos 21, tel. 3234357, fax 3225244, 162 b.
Family type hotel, good value, quiet yet in the centre of the Pláka, in a street with hotels. Good interior for a C-class hotel. Roof garden. Top rooms have a view of the Acropolis.

Attalos, Athinas 29, tel. 3212801/3, fax 3243124, 155 b.
Older, renovated hotel on the noisy market street between the Omónia and Monastiráki Squares. The rooms at the back are quiet. Nearly all the rooms have balconies with a view of the Acropolis. Roof terrace.

⋆Austria, Múson 7, tel. 9235151, fax 9247350, 71 b.
Intimate, small hotel, around a 15 minute walk from the Pláka. View of the Acropolis and the Philopáppos hill.

⋆Claridge, Dóru 4, tel. 522301393, 93 b.
Not very quietly located, but pleasant hotel on the Omónia Square.

⋆Hermes, Apóllonos 19, tel. 3235514, 85 b.
Quiet Hotel in the centre of the Pláka with lots of personal attention and

a family atmosphere. From the chain "Luxus-Creta-Maris". The Pláka nightlife is right outside your door.

Hotels in the wider area of Athens

Glyfáda
Palmyra Beach, A, Vass. Georgiu 70, tel. 8945808, 8981183, fax 8948110, 95 b., SP.
Modern hotel, 50m from the beach, soundproof windows.

Sea View, B, Xanthu 4, tel. 8947681, fax 9942189, 141 b., SP.
Built in 1973, renovated in 1995. Rooms with balcony.

Piraeus
Kastella, Kastella, B, Vassiléos Pávlu 75, tel. 4114735–7, fax 4175716, 48 b.
Small and pleasant family type hotel near the sea.

Bella Vista, Kastella, C, Vassiléos Pávlu 109, tel. 4113694, 69 b.
Small hotel on a hill above the yachting port of Mikrolímano; panoramic view of Athens and the Hymettós. Air conditioned rooms with large baths.

★Astir Palace, L, tel. 8960211, fax 8963194, 8962582.
Lovely location, famous beach. However, there is some air traffic noise. It consists of three large hotel buildings (Aphrodite, Nafsikia and Arion) and 72 smaller bungalows on a rocky peninsula. The more recent Aphrodite and Nafsikia offer spacious, modern rooms with balconies and terraces. The older, renovated Arion has pleasant rooms: numbers 153, 253 and 353 have corner balconies with a wonderful view of the Aegean Sea. Bathing coves with pebbly beach. Wide range of water sports. Health centre.

Information

National Tourist Organisation of Greece (EOT)

United Kingdom
44 Conduit Street, London WIR 8OJ
Tel. (020) 77345997, fax 72871369

United States
Olympic Tower, 645 Fifth Avenue, New York, NY 10022
Tel. (212) 421/5777, fax 8266940

West Sixth Street, Los Angeles, CA 90017
Tel. (213) 6266696, fax 4899744

North Michigan Avenue, Chicago, IL 60601
Tel. (312) 7821084, fax 7821091

Canada
1233 Rue de la Montagne
Montreal, Quebec H3B 2C9
Tel. (514) 8711498

Australia
51 Pitt St, Sydney
Tel. 2411663

Athens
Head Office
Amerikis 2
Tel. 3223111/9
Open Mon.–Fri. 12am–2.30pm

Information bureau in the National Bank building, Sýntagma Square, Karageorgi Servias 2
Tel. 3222545
Open: 9am–8pm

Information bureau,
Ermu 1
Tel: 3252267/8

Advance ticket sales
Vukurestiou 1; tel. 3234467
Open: 8am–2pm and 5–8pm

Ellinikó International Airport (Eastern Terminal)
Tel. 9702395/9799500
Open: 9am–8pm

Piraeus Office
Marina Zeas, E.O.T. Bldg; tel. 4135716/30, fax 4513623
Open: 9am–4pm

Further information can also be obtained from the tourist police in   Tourist Police
Athens (Sýngrou 7) and in other towns and districts. In the Athens area
dial 171.

Railway Travel Service (OSE), Karólou 1–3; tel. 5222491   Rail services
Agency at Larissa station; tel. 8213882
Railway timetable (recorded); tel. 145 (national), 147 (international)

Bus timetable (recorded); tel. 142   Bus services

Aegean: Harbour Office, Piraeus; tel. 4511311   Boat services
Express boats in Saronic Gulf; tel. 4527107, 4523612
Boat and ferry timetable (recorded); tel. 143

Language

In most parts of Greece visitors are likely to come across local people
with some knowledge of English or another European language; but in
the remoter areas and away from the tourist centres it is helpful to have
at least a smattering of modern Greek.

Modern Greek is considerably different from ancient Greek, though it is   Modern Greek
surprising to find how many words are still spelled the same way as in
classical times. Even in such cases, however, the pronunciation is likely
to be very different (see table). This difference in pronunciation is found
in both the main forms of modern Greek, dimotiki (demotic or popular
Greek) and katharévousa (the "purer" official or literary language).
   All official announcements, signs, timetables, etc. and the political
pages in newspapers are written in katharévousa, which approximates
more closely to classical Greek and may be deciphered, with some effort
perhaps, by those who learned Greek at school.
   The ordinary spoken language is demotic. This form, the result of a
long process of organic development, has now also established itself in
modern Greek literature, and is used in the lighter sections of newspapers.
   The differences between katharévousa and demotic are differences
both of grammar and vocabulary.

Greek alphabet

Letter		Anc. Greek	Mod. Greek	Pronunciation
A	α	alpha	alfa	a, semi-long
B	β	beta	vita	v
Γ	γ	gamma	gamma	g; y before e or i

137

Δ δ	delta	delta	dh as in English "the"
Ε ε	epsilon	épsilon	e, open, as in "egg"
Ζ ζ	zeta	zita	z
Η η	eta	ita	ee, semi-long
Θ θ	theta	thita	th as in "thin"
Ι ι	iota	iota	ee, semi-long
Κ κ	kappa	kappa	k
Λ λ	lambda	lamdha	l
Μ μ	mu	mi	m
Ν ν	nu	ni	n
Ξ ξ	xi	xi	ks
Ο ο	omicron	ómikron	o, open, semi-long
Π π	pi	pi	p
Ρ ρ	rho	ro	r, lightly rolled
Σ σ	sigma	sigma	s
Τ τ	tau	taf	t
Υ υ	ypsilon	ípsilon	ee, semi-long
Φ φ	phi	fi	f
Χ χ	chi	khi	kh, ch as in "loch"; before e or i, somewhere between kh and sh
Ψ ψ	psi	psi	ps
Ω ω	omega	oméga	o, open, semi-long

Accents

The position of the stress in a word is very variable, but is always shown in the Greek alphabet by an accent, either acute ('), grave (`) or circumflex (ˆ); since there is no difference in modern Greek between the three types of accent, the acute is used in this guide to indicate stress.

Punctuation

The "breathings" over a vowel or dipthong at the beginning of a word, whether rough (') or smooth ('), are not pronounced. The diaeresis (¨) over a vowel indicates that it is to be pronounced separately, and not as part of a dipthong. Punctuation marks are the same as in English, except that the semi-colon (;) is used in place of the question mark (?) and a point above the line (·) in place of the semicolon.

Numbers

Cardinals

0	midén
1	éna
2	dío
3	tria
4	téssera
5	pénde
6	éksi
7	eftá
8	okhtó
9	enneá
10	déka
11	éndeka
12	dódeka
13	dekatrís
14	dekatéssera
15	dekapénde
16	dekaéksi
17	dekaëftá
18	dekaokhtó
19	dekaënneá
20	íkosi
21	íkosi éna
22	íkosi dío
30	triánda

31	triánda éna
40	saránda
50	penínda
60	eksínda
70	evdomínda
80	ogdónda
90	enenínda
100	ekató
101	ekató énas, miá, éna
153	ekató penínda tría
200	diakósia
300	triakósia
400	tetrakósia
500	pendakósia
600	eksakósia
700	eftakósia
800	okhtakósia
900	enneakósia
1000	khília
5000	pénde khiliádes
1,000,000	éna ekatommírio

1st	prótos, próti, próto(n)	Ordinals
2nd	défteros, -i, -o(n)	
3rd	trítos, -i, -o(n)	
4th	tétartos, -i, -o(n)	
5th	pémptos	
6th	éktos	
7th	évdomos	
8th	ógdoos	
9th	énnatos	
10th	dékatos	
11th	endékatos	
20th	ikostós	
30th	triakostós	
100th	ekatostós	
124th	ekatostós ikostós tétartos	
1000th	khiliostós	

½	misós, -i, -ó (n), ímisis	Fractions
⅓	tríton	
¼	tétarton	
⅒	dékaton	

Everyday Expressions

Good morning, good day!	Kaliméra!
Good evening!	Kalispéra!
Good night!	Kali nikhta!
Goodbye!	Adío!
Do you speak English?	Omilíte angliká?
German?	yermaniká?
French?	ghalliká?
I do not understand	Dhe sas katalaváno
Excuse me	Signómi!
Yes	Nè (turning head to side)
No	Ókhi (jerking head upwards)
Please	Parakaló
Thank you	Efkharistó
Yesterday	Khthes
Today	Símera
Tomorrow	Ávrio (n)
Help!	Voítha!

Language

Open	Aniktó
When?	Póte?
Single room	Dhomátio mè éna kreváti
Double room	Dhomátio mè dhío krevátia
Room with a bath	Dhomátio mè lutró
What does it cost?	Pósso káni?
Wake me at 6 o'clock	Ksipníste me stis eksi
Where is ...	Pu íne ...
the toilet?	i toualéta?
a pharmacy?	éna pharmakío?
a doctor?	énas yatró?
a dentist?	énas odhondoyatrós?
... Street?	o odhós (+ name in Genitive)
... Square?	i platía (+ name in Genitive)

Travelling	Aerodrome, airfield	Aerodhromío
	Aircraft	Aeropláno
	Airport	Aerolimín
	All aboard!	Is tas théses sas!
	Arrival	Áfiksi
	Bank	Trápeza
	Boat	Várka
	Bus	Leoforío
	Change	Alásso
	Departure (by air)	Apoyíosi
	Exchange (money)	Alají Xrimáton
	Ferry	Férri-bóut
	Flight	Ptísi
	Hotel	Ksenodhokhío
	Information	Pliroforía
	Lavatory/bathroom	Toualéta
	Luggage	Aposkevás
	Luggage check	Apódhiksis ton aposkevón
	Non-smoking compartment	Dhya mi kapnistás
	Platform	Grammí
	Porter	Akhthofóros
	Railway	Sidhiródhromos
	Railway station	Statmós
	Restaurant car	Vagóni estiatoríu
	Ship	Karávi, plíon
	Sleeping-car	Vagón-li, klinámaska
	Smoking compartment	Dhya kapnistás
	Stop (bus)	Stási
	Taxi	Taksí
	Ticket	Isitírio
	Ticket collector	Ispráktor
	Ticket-window	Thíris
	Timetable	Dhromolóyio
	Train	Tréno
	Waiting room	Ethusa anamonis
	Youth hostel	Ksenónas néon

Post office	Address	Dhiéfthinsi
	Air mail	Aeroporikós
	Express	Epíyon ghrámma
	Letter	Ghrámma
	Letter-box	Ghrammatokivótio
	Package	Dhematáki
	Parcel	Dhéma, pakétto
	Postcard	Takhidromikí kárta
	Poste restante	Post restánt
	Post office	Takhidhromíon
	Registered	Sistiméno ghrámma

Stamp	Ghrammatósimo(n)	
Telegram	Tileghráfima	
Telephone	Tiléfono (n)	
Telex	Tilépeto (n)	
Monday	Dheftéra	Days of the week
Tuesday	Tríti	
Wednesday	Tetárti	
Thursday	Pémpti	
Friday	Paraskeví	
Saturday	Sávato(n)	
Sunday	Kiriakí	
Day	(I)méra	
Weekday	Katheriminí	
Holiday	Skholí	
Week	Evdhomádha	
New Year's Day	Protokhroniá	Holidays
Easter	Páskha	
Whitsun	Pendikostí	
Christmas	Khristúyenna	
January	Yanuários	Months
February	Fevruários	
March	Mártios	
April	Aprílios	
May	Máyos	
June	Yúnios	
July	Yúlios	
August	Ávghustos	
September	Septémvrios	
October	Októvrios	
November	Noémvrios	
December	Dhekémvrios	
Month	Mínas	

Media

Newspapers (efimerida, periodikó)

British newspapers (efimerida, periodikó) are available at street kiosks in central Athens.

The English language newspaper "Athens News" and the weekly "This Week in Athens" contain information that is of interest to tourists, such as exchange rates, weather reports and programmes of events. A monthly English language magazine "Athenion" is also published.

Television

International films are often shown in the original language with Greek sub-titles. Satellite stations SAT 1 and RTL also broadcast programmes.

Motoring

The speed limit for passenger vehicles, including trailers, is: Traffic regulations
50 k.p.h. (31 m.p.h.) built-up areas
80 k.p.h. (50 m.p.h.) ordinary roads
100 k.p.h. (62 m.p.h.) motorways and expressways

The limit for motorcycles is 70 k.p.h. (43 m.p.h.) on all roads.
Parking is not permitted where there are yellow lines painted by the roadside and on roads that have priority.

Tolls	Tolls are payable on some motorways and expressways.
Information	ELPA (Automobile and Touring Club of Greece) Odós Messógion 2–4; tel. 7791615 Information about road conditions.
Breakdown service	ELPA; tel. 104. The breakdown service operates over a radius of 60 km (37 mi.) from Athens. Call out and towing charges are payable. The main tourist routes are patrolled from April to September by the yellow vehicles of the ELPA breakdown service, marked "Assistance Routiäre". Drivers in need of assistance should indicate this by raising the bonnet of their car or waving a yellow cloth.
Insurance	Visitors travelling by car should ensure that their insurance is comprehensive and covers use of the vehicle in Europe. See also Travel Documents.

Museums

Opening hours

Most museums are open five days a week 9am–3pm. Many are closed at the beginning of the week (mostly Monday and Tuesday).

Most archaeological sites and museums are closed on the following days: January 1st, March 25th, Good Friday, Easter Sunday, December 25th and 26th.

Sunday opening times operate on the following days: Epiphany, Lent Monday, Easter Saturday and Sunday, May 1st, Whit Sunday, August 15th, October 28th.

Opening times are subject to alteration so it is advisable to check with the National Tourist Office for Greece (see Information); tel. 3222545 and 3223111.

Admission fees are levied at most museums and archaeological sites.

Nightlife

See Baedeker Special p. 144

Opening Hours

Banks	Mon.–Thu. 8am–2pm, Fri. 8am–1.30pm. Banks at Sýntagma Square and Piraeus and branches of some of the larger banks may stay open later.
Chemists	Mon., Wed., Sat. 8.30am–2.30pm, Tue., Thu., Fri. 8.30am–1.30pm, 5–8pm.
Museums	See entry
Post offices	See Post
Shops	Shops are usually open Mon., Wed., Sat. 8am–2.30pm, Tue., Thu., Fri. 8am–1.30pm, 5–8pm Tourist souvenir shops are open in the evenings Mon.–Sat. See also Public Holidays.

Post

Eólu and corner of Mitropóleos and Sýntagma Square, open Mon.–Fri. 7.30am–8pm, Sat. 8am–2pm (Syntagma also Sun, 9am–1pm)

Main post offices

The smaller post offices in the suburbs are open Mon.–Fri. 7.30am–1pm.

Small post offices

Kumundúru (near the National Theatre) and Stadiu 4 (in the arcades) Open: Mon.–Fri. 7.30am–2.15pm, Sat. 7.30am–2.15pm, Sun. 9am–1.30pm Packets and registered letters must be presented open for inspection before 1.30pm.

Parcel post

Letters and postcards sent within the EU (maximum 20 grams) cost 140 dr.

Postal tariffs

Each area of Athens has a five figure post code beginning with 1.

Athens post code

Public Holidays

New Year's Day (January 1st), Epiphany (January 6th), Independence Day (March 25th), May Day (May 1st), Ochi Day (October 28th; "No" Day, commemorating the Greek rejection of the Italian ultimatum in 1940), Christmas Day and Boxing Day (December 25th and 26th).

Statutory holidays

The most important are: Katharí Deftéra (Lent Monday), Good Friday Easter (According to the Orthodox Church Easter coincides with the western churches only every four years. In Greece it is celebrated from one to four weeks later than in Central Europe.), Whitsun, The Assumption, The Annunciation.
   Most public institutions and shops are closed on the mornings of January 2nd and 5th, the last Saturday of Lent, the Thursday before Easter and Easter Saturday. There are also local religious festivals (*panigiri*) and saints' days.

Religious days

Public Transport

Buses are the main form of public transport within Athens with some trolley buses operating on certain inner city routes.
   A light railway system "Elektrikós" (partly underground) links Piraeus with the northern suburb of Kifissiá.

Public transport is free of charge 5–8am. A single fare at other times is 75 dr. and it is useful to have the correct fare ready. When changing buses the fare of 75 dr. must be paid again.

Fares

The Athens underground/light railway system "Elektrikós" bisects the city from north to south (see map page 147). It operates at ten minute intervals between 5am and midnight.

Elektrikós

Yellow trolley buses operate in the city centre. Tickets (75 dr.) can be purchased from kiosks.

Trolley buses

The network of city bus lines (blue-white buses) covers the entire area of Greater Athens. Termini are Mount Párnes in the north, Kastri in the north-east, Loutsa in the east, Varkiza in the south-east, Piraeus in the south-west and Dafni in the west. Buses operate on most routes at reg-

Blue-white city buses

Long Nights in Athens

A social get-together, sharing a drink or two, are today an essential ingredient of Greek culture and lifestyle. In the earliest days it was already considered to be good practice to enjoy your food and drink together with others, although the symposium (syn + posis = together drinking) only became an institution in the life of free citizens after the 5th century BC. The ancient Greeks, of course, were able to indulge their pleasures with far less restraint for, unlike their compatriots today, they did not have to go to work the morning after – that was done for them by the slaves. No wonder then, that the symposium was not an exceptional event in antiquity but a normal part of everyday life in Greece...

And today? The opportunities for whiling away the nights in Athens are manifold and certainly not restricted to the old town Pláka. Some are drawn first to the theatre or cinema and then to a restaurant, others start off straightaway in the taverna and afterwards choose a bar, a club or a pub with live music. No matter which of the numerous variations one chooses – for each one there is an abundance of addresses. In Kifissiá, for example, the café-bar *Tesseris Epoches* invites with its coffee-house atmosphere and relaxing music in an old mansion house. In Agia Paraskevi it is the *Alba* with its beautiful garden and a gallery on the first floor as well as live music; near the centre, you can enjoy the gallery, live music and very good and well-priced food in the renovated royal stables of the *Stavlos*.

For a coffee at lunchtime or a drink in the evening the *To Bajoko* is a great place, situated in the centre. If you want to be 'trendy' and don't mind having your drink while standing,

you'll feel comfortable in the *Vaila* (Baila) in one of the pedestrianised zones in the elegant area Kolónaki. Of the numerous beer halls in town, the *Bitten fatten* in Kifissiá can be recommended. Here the guest has a choice of seven draught and 120 bottled beers. Besides, the food is excellent here, too. Excellent coffee and sweet pastries can be found right in the centre of Piraeus, in Passalimani, in the recently opened Café *De Luka*.

A good address for a meal is the *Caprice* in the elegant quarter Kolónaki. You have a choice of three rooms: the first one with its subdued music is the best place to enjoy the excellent food, the second one serves as a bar, and in the third one you can round off the evening with a coffee and a sweet. At lunchtime, inexpensive snacks are served here, in the evening, international dishes with a Mediterranean slant. There are no house wines, but instead excellent bottled wines; and all this for a decent price (a complete menu for two costs about £30). For typically Greek food of the highest standard and excellent wines from the barrel you could go to the taverna *Avgo tou Kokora* (open from 11am until dawn; dinner for two is about £16) in the district Kipseli, close to the centre. If you like to have a selection of different dishes in small portions on the table, you are best served at a 'Mezedopolia' (mezedes = starters), for example at the *Athinaiko*, founded in 1932, right in the heart of the city. The *Kantaras* is an old-style bistro which serves a delicious Nemea wine and the cuisine of Asia Minor. Equally well known for its mezedes is the *Achinos* in Piraeus, Passalimani, a restaurant with sea view and an impressive selection of delicious fish and seafood starters.

If you'd like to experience where

better-off Athenian ladies indulge in a bit of Greek light entertainment, you should aim for one of the numerous 'bouzoukia', but expect steep prices, programmes starting around midnight and, especially at weekends, thronging crowds – you will, however, gain a deep insight into the Greek spirit! Of this type of bar, which can be found all over town but especially in the Syngru, the *Vio-Vio* and the *Medusa* are worth recommending.

If you fancy 'clubbing', make your way to the Leofóros Vuliagmenis which leads from the centre to the airport. Here you'll find a large number of clubs catering for a variety of musical tastes. The *Camel Club* hides at number 268; Fridays and Saturdays are the liveliest nights here. The club, with its impressive interior design – and equally impressive admission prices – stretches over two levels.

If you want to experience good Greek music in a relaxed atmosphere you can find a suitable bar in the Pláka, for example the *Esperides* or – with Rembetiko – the *Aperitto*. If you prefer jazz, rock or Latin American music, you'd be better placed at the *Public*. Pure Rembetika can be experienced at the *Ta Rembetika*, while the *To Baraki tou Vassili* offers an interesting mixture of live music without microphone, theatre performances and short films. Every Monday night, old Greek music is played, Tuesdays are reserved for Pontic evenings and, on Fridays, music from Smirni and Rembetika can be enjoyed.

A night of drinking and dancing demands to be rounded off in a suitable way. On Omónia Square, for example, there is a whole range of shops that sell coffee and sandwiches as well as kiosks that offer a supply of the latest papers. If your stomach cries out for something more substantial, then follow the Greek example and eat a Patzas soup early in the morning (a soup made from pig's head, feet and offal, flavoured with vinegar) – for example at the *Lefkos Pirgos* in Acharnon street in the centre, off Victoria Square.

Even if you feel the urge to go shopping in the middle of the night, Athens has the place for you: Jorgos' little supermarket in the Ippokratus opens 24 hours.

Café bars:

Tesseris Epoches, Kifissiá, Platía Agiu Dimitriu (open 9am to 1.30am)
Alba, Agia Paraskevi, Agios Ioannu/ Asimakopulu 3
Stavlos, near the centre, Iraklidon 10, Thissíon (open 12pm to midnight)
To Bajoko, centre, Ippokratus 146 (open lunchtime to midnight)
Vaila, Kolónaki, Haritos 43
De Luka, Piraeus, Passalimani
Beer hall Bitten Fatten, Kifissiá, Platía Agios Dimitriu 17

Restaurants:

Caprice, Kolónaki, Iraklitu/Fokilidu
Athinaiko, centre, Themistokleus 2
Kantaras, centre, Ermú 99/Normanu (open lunchtime and evening)
Achinos, Piraeus, Passalimani, Akti Themistokleos 51, Tel. 452 69 44
Avgo tu Kokora, Kipseli, Sporadon 40, Tel. 822 88 40

Bouzoukia:

Vio-Vio, Syngrú 137 (expensive)
Medusa, Makri 2, Makrijanni

Live music:

Esperides, Tholu 6 (admission from 10pm)
Aperitto, Kolónaki, Dimokritus 25
Public, Chatzigianni Mexi 6
Ta Rembetika, Neos Kosnos, Karpou 49
To Baraki tou Vassili, centre, Zoodochu Pigis 98, Tel.: 381 53 45 (start after 11pm)

ular intervals between 6am and 11pm. The fare of 75 dr. is thrown into the cash box located next to the driver.

Green express buses

Green express buses operate on certain routes. The most important is No. 040, which runs every 10 minutes throughout the 24 hours from Athens (Filellinon) to Piraeus.

Orange buses

Orange buses operate between Athens and important destinations in Attica. The fare is collected on board by a conductor.
Important stops are:
Platia Egyptou (end of Alexandras Street; buses to Lavrion and Soúnion via Markopulo or along the coast).
Mavromateion ("Green Park"; buses to Marathón, Nea Makri and Ráfina).

Airport buses

See Air Travel

Important bus stations

Acharnon: direction of Párnes
Kaningos, Omónia: direction Halandri, Marussi, Psychiko, Kifissiá
Thission: direction of Lútsa, east Attica
Zappion: direction of Glyfáda, Vula, Vuliagméni, Varkiza
Eleftherias (Kumunduru), Pireos: direction of Dafni, Eleusis
Kiffissou 100: overland buses to Corinth, Lutraki, Mycaenae, Epidaurus and other towns on the Peloponnese.
Liossion 260: overland buses to Delphi and other places in central and Northern Greece.

Signs

Destinations and other signs are usually written in Greek script:

Entrance = ΕΙΣΟΔΟΣ
Exit = ΕΞΟΔΟΣ
Stop signal (press bell above exit doors) = ΣΤΑΣΗ

To inform the driver to stop at the next bus stop shout "Stássis!" loudly.

Railway stations

Trains depart from Laríssis station (stathmós Laríssis) to Central and Northern Greece.
Information: tel. 8213882
   Trains of the narrow-gauge Peloponnese Railway (SPAP) depart from the nearby Peloponnese station to Corinth, Pátras, Trípolis and Kalamata.
Information: tel. 5131601
   Piraeus station is the terminus for the Greek National Railway and the Peloponnese Railway.
Information: tel. 4178335

Restaurants

Tavernas

Bakiria, Mavromicháli 119 (Sun. closed).
Popular with students. Offers a wide choice of salads.

Europe, Omónia, Satovriándu 7.
Old fashioned, with high ceilings. On the menu you will find Patsá and roast lamb head.

Filippu, Kolonáki, Xenokrátus 18 (Sun. closed).
This well known taverna lies on the foot of the Lykabettós hill, offering wonderful views. The menu offers fine traditional dishes.

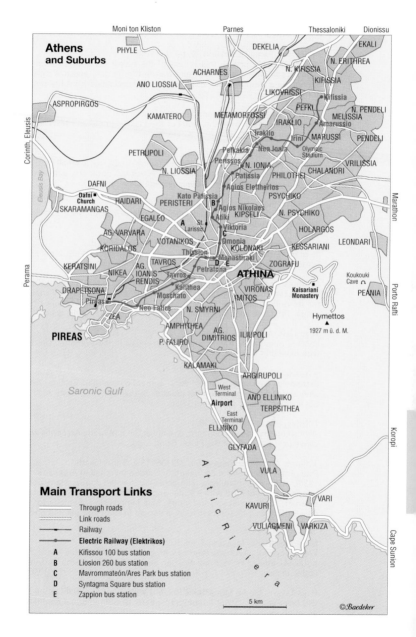

Athens
and Suburbs

Moni ton Kliston   Parnes   Thessaloniki   Dionissu

PHYLE   DEKELIA   EKALI
ACHARNES   N. KIFISSIA   N. ERITHREA
ANO LIOSSIA   KIFISSIA
ASPROPIRGOS   LIKOVRISSI   Kifissia
KAMATERO   METAMORFOSSI   PEFKI   N. PENDELI
IRAKLIO   MELISSIA
PETRUPOLI   Iraklio   Amarussio
Irini   MARUSSI   PENDELI
Pefkakia   Nea Jonia   Olympic   VRILISSIA
Perissos   Stadium
N. LIOSSIA   N. IONIA   PHILOTHEI   CHALANDRI
DAFNI   Patissia
Dafni   Agios Eleftherios   PSYCHIKO
Church   Kato Patissia
HAIDARI   PERISTERI   **B**   Agios Nikolaos
SKARAMANGAS   Atiki   KIPSELI   N. PSYCHIKO
EGALEO   **A**   St.   HOLARGOS
AG. VARVARA   Larissis   Viktoria   LEONDARI
VOTANIKOS   Omonia   KESSARIANI
KORIDALOS   Thission   KOLONAKI
KERATSINI   AG.   TAVROS   Monastiraki   ZOGRAFU   Koukouki
NIKEA   IOANIS   Tavros   **D E**   Cave
RENDIS   Petralona   **ATHINA**
DRAPETSONA   Kalithea   VIRONAS   Kaisariani   PEANIA
Piraes   Moschato   IMITOS   Monastery
ZEA   Neo Faliro   N. SMYRNI   Hymettos
PIREAS   AMPHITHEA   AG.   1927 m ü. d. M.
P. FALIRO   DIMITRIOS   ILIUPOLI
KALAMAKI
ARGIRUPOLI
West
Terminal   ANO ELLINIKO
Saronic Gulf   **Airport**   TERPSITHEA
East
Terminal
ELLINIKO
GLYFADA
VULA
VARI
KAVURI
VULIAGMENI   VARKIZA

Corinth, Eleusis
Eleusis Bay
Perama
Marathon
Porto Rafti
Koropi
Cape Sunion

Attic Riviera

Main Transport Links

	Through roads
	Link roads
	Railway
	Electric Railway (Elektrikos)
A	Kifissou 100 bus station
B	Liosion 260 bus station
C	Mavrommateón/Ares Park bus station
D	Syntagma Square bus station
E	Zappion bus station

5 km

©Baedeker

Restaurants

Fondas, Adrannitu 6.
Also located at the Lykabettós hill. Serves wine from wooden casks. The
chef will gladly let you have a peek in his cooking pot.

★Karavitis, Pangráti, Arktínu 10, tel. 7215155
Very reasonably priced, this is one of the oldest tavernas in Athens.
Richly traditional, with a tall palm tree in the garden, and live music.
Serves wine from wooden casks and meat specialities from the wood
burning grill.

O Damigos, Pláka, Kidathinéon (closed in mid summer).
Ethnic cellar taverna, in the heart of the Pláka. Simple and tasty food,
wine from wooden casks.

O Platanos, Pláka, Diogénus (Sun. closed).
Richly traditional, romantic taverna (since 1932), in a small hidden
corner of the Pláka. In summer food is served outdoors, wine from
wooden casks. Traditional dishes, average price range.

Peristeria, Pláka, Patrú 5A.
Richly traditional taverna but with a modern interior, with excellent
Retsina from wooden casks.

Rodia, Kolonáki, Aristíppu 44, tel. 3220666 (Sun. closed).
In a romantic old house with a small roof garden. Wide choice of
starters, for example squid salad. Mainly younger clientele.

Sokrates' Prison, Makrigianni, Mitséon 20, tel. 9223434 (Sun. closed).
Elegant taverna, located behind the Odeion Herodes Atticus. Well known
for its grill specialities and wine from wooden casks. Average price
range. Tip: lamb chops with mushrooms, potatoes and garlic sauce.

Thanassis, Ambókipi, Kandánu.
Located outside the town centre. Guitar music in the evenings. Garden
with olive and fig trees.

★Tsekura, Pláka, Tripódon3.
Extremely well established, very authentic taverna. Retsina from
wooden casks. Lots of regular guests. Simple but very tasty dishes.
Specialities: stífado and squid salad.

Thespis, Pláka, Théspidos 18.
With a countryside atmosphere, directly at the foot of the Acropolis with
views over the roofs of the Pláka. Good food.

★Xynos, Angelu Geronta 4, tel. 3221065 (Sat./Sun. closed).
One of the oldest and most beautiful Garden tavernas in Athens (since
1935), with wall paintings, characteristic for the Pláka. Many local
people. Excellent food with a wide range of dishes, music equally characteristic for the Pláka. Good value. Milk lamb dishes. Famous for its
dessert Chalvas. In sommer food is served in the large planted courtyard.

Manessis, Márku Mussúru 3, tel. 9227684.
Well loved typical Athens taverna with garden. Sophisticated level. Live
bousouki music. Wine from wooden casks. Speciality: lamb and veg-
etable dishes.

Palia Tavern, Márku Mussúru 35, tel. 9029493 (Sun. closed).
Old taverna (since 1896) full of atmosphere. Good traditional food. Live
vocal music.

Restaurants

Aerides, Pláka, Avrilíu 3.
Here you'll dine in the rooms of a house from the 19th century.

★Bajazzo, Tyrteu 1, tel. 9213012 (Sun. closed).
Stylish restored neoclassical patrician villa near the Acropolis. The German chef produces the finest Greek dishes, which come at a price.

Balthazar, Ambelókipi, Vurnazu 14, tel. 6441215.
This expensive brasserie and bar is located in a classical villa with a palm tree garden. Fantastic cocktails. Speciality: pepper steak.

★Bouillabaisse, Pireus, Kumundúru 58.
Restaurant on the Pireus port of Mikrolímano. Specializes in fresh seafood.

Canaris, Pireus, Kumundúru 50.
This fish restaurant is famous for its crayfish and octopus specialities.

★Delfi, Nikis 13, tel. 3234869, 3228114 (Sun. closed).
Favoured by the local population, this is one of the best restaurants in town. Close to Syntágma Square. High price level. Excellent food with an extensive choice of dishes.

Dionisos, Lykabettós
Exclusive restaurant on the town mountain of Lykabettós.

Eden, Lissiu 12, tel. 3248858 (Tues. closed).
First vegetarian restaurant in Athens. Tasty, imaginative dishes. Tip: stuffed aubergine.

Wonderful view of Athens by night from restaurant Dionisos on the Lykabettós

★Gerofínikas, Kolonáki, Pindaru 10, tel. 3636710.
Respected, classical Greek restaurant, highly rated. At the end of a long passage way. Favoured by tourists and business people. Greek dishes like you won't find anywhere else, oriental specialities and excellent desserts.

Kastellorizo, Thiseos 230–234.
Excellent fish restaurant, very popular with the locals.

★Myrtia, Trivoniánu 32–34, tel. 9023633 (Sun. closed).
Famous and expensive top restaurant, often visited by politicians. Live music. Excellent starters and main courses. Extensive wine cellar.

O Anthropos, Pangráti, Archélau 13 (Sun. closed).
Very original and sophisticated fish restaurant with extaordinary creations. Speciality: Squid à la Onassis.

Posidon, Pláka, Kapnikaréas 35–39.
Lovely restaurant on a square near the Roman Agorá.

Psaropulos, Glifáda, Kalamón 2.
Fish restaurant on the yachting port.

★Trata O Stelios, Käsarianí, Annagenníseos 7–9.
Good fish restaurant in working class area of Käsarianí.

Shopping

Opening hours See entry

Ermou

You can buy anything in the Pláka

Ermou, which links Sýntagma Square with Monastiráki Square, is the main shopping street in Athens together with Evangelistrias and Ajiu Markou. Clothes, leather and household goods are on sale as well as copperware, handicrafts and furniture.

Flea market

There is a large flea market around Monastiráki Square on Sunday mornings.

Pláka

Almost everything can be found in Pláka and on the Makrigiani (south-east) below the Acropolis. Numerous shops are open until late at night. Every kind of souvenir, natural sponges, silver filigree, flokati rugs, icons, copper and pewter goods, articles made of marble, alabaster and onyx and foodstuffs are for sale. Lower prices can be obtained by haggling in the Eastern fashion.

The shops around Kolonáki Square, the centre of the former diplomatic quarter, specialise in luxury goods. Well known couturiers, shops selling leather goods, jewellers' and galleries are to be found here.

Kolonáki

Here, too, can be found a great range of goods with prices lower than those around Sýntagma Square.

Omónai Square

Athinas Street runs through the middle of the market quarter with the various kinds of shop concentrated in particular streets.The Athens meat market is situated between Sofokleos and Evripidu. It provides an unusual sight for visitors from Central and Northern Europe.

Athinas

Prices in Piraeus are slightly cheaper than in the city centre. Trúmba is the lively centre of Piraeus, once renowned as the red-light area.
   Beside the harbour are many shops selling all kinds of goods catering to the tourists visiting the islands.

Piraeus

The most popular souvenirs are textiles, woven goods, fashionable fur coats, leather goods, ceramics, gold and silverwork, jewellery, articles made from marble, alabaster, onyx, copper and pewter, icons, olives, dried fruits, nuts and wine.

Souvenirs

Good quality products are available at reasonable prices from the following outlets:
Benaki Museum shop
Centre of Hellenic Art & Tradition, Pláka, Pandrossou 36
Greek Women's Institution, Vukurestiu 13
Lyceum of Greek Women, Dimokritou 17
Branches of the National Charity Organisation, Vukurestiou and Kolonáki
XAN (YMCA) Shop, Amerikis

Folk art and crafts

The export from Greece of antiquities and works of art dated before 1830 is forbidden. An export licence must be issued before valuable antiques (archaiótetes) can be exported. For ecumenical items this is available from the Byzantine Museum and from the National Gallery for secular items.
   There are no restrictions on buying and exporting copies of ancient exhibits, such as are on sale in the National Archaeological Museum of Athens.
   Most vases and urns must be washed with care as the colours are not usually fixed, not having been fired.

Antiques

Sport

Greek Cycling Federation, Liosion 123; tel. 8831414

Cycling

Glyfáda Golf Club, near the eastern terminal of Athens airport; tel. 8946875 Hellenic Golf Club, Varibombi near Kifissiá

Golf

Greek Riding Club, Marússi, Paradisou 18; tel. 6812506
Athens Riding Club, Gérakas, Ajia Paraskevi; tel. 6611088
Hippodrom, Faliron, end of Syngrú; tel. 941 77 61; races Mon., Wed., Sat. from 2.30pm.

Riding

Greek Sailing Association, Poseidonas St; tel. 9304827/8

Sailing

Taxis

Marinas, yachting and sailing clubs at Piraeus (Mikrolimano, Zea), Páleo Fáliron (Flisvos), Glyfáda, Vuliagméni and Alimos.
Information brochure (published annually):"Greece for Yachtsmen", from the National Tourist Organisation of Greece.

Sea fishing | Information from the harbour master's office at Piraeus; tel. 4511311/9

Surfing | Hellenic Wind Surfing Association, Filellinon 7; tel. 3233606
Equipment is available for hire from beaches maintained by the National Tourist Organisation of Greece and from surfing schools.

Tennis | There are tennis courts in all parts of the city.

Walking | Association of Greek Walking Clubs, Dragatsaniu; tel. 3234107

Water-skiing | Water-skiing Club, Sturnara 32; tel. 5231875

Stadia | See Sights from A to Z, Stadion; Olympic Sportsground; Peace and Friendship Stadium

Taxis

There are taxis everywhere in Athens. They can be found in busy public places (airports, railway stations, Piraeus harbour, Sýntagma Square, Omónia Square, bus stations, etc.) and in front of large hotels and museums. They can also be hailed by shouting or waving from the edge of the road. Taxis operate throughout the 24 hours. Only taxis bearing the letter Z are permitted to drive in the city centre on even-numbered days and those with the letter M on odd-numbered days.

Fares | Athens taxis have meters. The basic hire charge is (1990) 240 dr. plus 62 dr. per kilometre within the Athens-Piraeus city area (extending to Ekáli, Pérama, Eleusis, Várkitsa and Agía Paraskeví). Additional charges apply from railway and bus stations, sea and airports, for pieces of luggage and for journeys between midnight and 5am.

Central taxi office | Tel. 8030130

Taxi ranks | Agía Paraskeví; tel. 6592444
Amurússion; tel. 8020818
Glyfáda; tel. 8944531
Kalamáki; tel. 9818103
Nea Erithrea; tel. 8013450
Kifissía underground station; tel. 8013373
Sýntagma Square; tel. 3237942
Psychiko; tel. 6718191
Piraeus; tel. 4178138

Telephone

International codes | From the UK to Athens: 00301
From the US or Canada to Athens: 011301
From Athens to the UK: 0044
From Athens to the US or Canada: 001

The zero at the beginning of the local code should be omitted for international calls.

Athens: tel. 131
Rest of Greece: tel. 132
International: tel. 161
General information on OTE: tel. 134

Directory
enquiries

Red telephones for local calls are installed in department stores, cafés and most kiosks.

Local calls

Time

Greece observes East European time, 2 hours ahead of Greenwich Mean Time.

Tipping

Hotel tariffs normally include a service charge.

Hotels

Restaurants usually include a service charge, but it is customary to leave a tip of 5–10 per cent.

Restaurants, cafés

In taxis it is usual to round up the amount paid to the driver by 10 per cent.

Taxis

Travel Documents

For a stay of up to three months a valid passport is required. For longer stays an extension must be applied for at the nearest police station at least 20 days before the end of the three-month period.

Personal
documents

British driving licences and registration documents are accepted in Greece. Drivers from most other countries must have an international driving licence.
An international insurance certificate ("green card") valid for Greece is required and an oval nationality plate must be displayed. Comprehensive insurance, though not compulsory, is recommended.

Vehicle
documents

When to Go

For the visitor from central and northern Europe the climate in Athens and Attica is most pleasant in spring and autumn. The months of March to May are mild and the trees are in bloom. The summer months are very hot, especially in the city. In September the temperatures become more pleasant again, with the first showers of rain in October.

Youth Hostels

Organosis Xenonon Neotitos Ellados (Greek Youth Hostel Association), Dargatsaniu 4, Platia Klafthmonos; tel. 3234167, 3237590

Information

International Youth Hostel, Victor Hugo 16; tel. 5234170, fax 5234015
Youth Hostel No. 5, Pagrati, Damareos 75; tel. 7519530, fax 7510616
Youth Hostel No. 2, Alexandros 87–89; tel. 6442421, 6426529

Youth hostels

153

Youth Hostels

XAN (YMCA)	Omirou 28; tel. 3626970
XEN (YWCA)	Amerikis 11; tel. 3626180

Guest houses (selection)	Dioscouri, Pittaku 6; tel. 3248165
	Josef House, M. Mossouri 13; tel. 9231204
	Marvel House, Zini 35; tel. 9234058
	Student Inn, Kydathineon 16; tel. 3244808

Index

Picture credits

Imprint

65 photographs, 18 maps and plans, 1 large town map

German text: Rainer Eisenschmid, Dr. Otto Gärtner, Reinhard Strüber

General direction: Baedeker-Redaktion (Carmen Galenschovski)

Cartography: Franz Huber, München; Mairs Geographischer Verlag, Ostfildern; Hallwag AG, Bern (large town map)

Editorial work: g-and-w PUBLISHING, Oxfordshire

English translation: David Cocking, Julie Waller, Sylvia Golding

Front cover: AA Photo Library (R. Surman)
Back cover: AA Photo Library (T. Harris)

3rd English edition 2000

© Baedeker Ostfildern
Original German edition 1999

© 2000 The Automobile Association
English language edition worldwide

Published by AA Publishing (a trading name of Automobile Association Developments Limited, whose registered office is Norfolk House, Priestley Road, Basingstoke, Hampshire RG24 9NY. Registered number 1878835).

Distributed in the United States and Canada by:
Fodor's Travel Publications, Inc.
201 East 50th Street
New York, NY 10022

A CIP catalogue record of this book is available from the British Library.
Licensed user: Mairs Geographischer Verlag GmbH & Co., Ostfildern

Typeset by Fakenham Photosetting Ltd
Printed in Italy by G. Canale & C. S.p.A., Turin

ISBN 0 7495 2406 5

Notes